THE PSYCHOLOGY OF RELIGIOUS EXPERIENCES

THE
PSYCHOLOGY
OF
RELIGIOUS
EXPERIENCES

Erwin Ramsdell Goodenough

BASIC BOOKS, INC., PUBLISHERS

NEW YORK

The dogmas of the quiet past are inadequate to the stormy present. The occasion is piled high with difficulty, and we must rise to the occasion. As our case is new, so we must think anew and act anew. We must disenthrall ourselves, and then we shall save our country.

—LINCOLN'S "CALL TO PRAYER," 1862

For CYNTHIA

Preface

WHAT IS POPULARLY CALLED the "psychology of religion" is a highly important matter which for long has fallen among various stools. Seventy years ago, both psychologists and anthropologists, most of whom had begun life with deep religious concern, were collecting and studying data on man's religious life in a way that is now little done. The growth of scientific thinking suddenly made general observations and approximate conclusions increasingly unattractive, and the data of religion did not lend themselves to precise or quantitative study. A new pattern, that of devotion to the precise appraisal of data, came into being among the intelligentsia, which scorned the old approaches as disdainfully as the prophets of Israel had scorned the idols of Baal, scorned them all the more because they themselves were not aware that they were setting up what they took to be the "true" faith, belief in counting and measuring, over against the old theological ones.

This new religion of the quest or search, of which I shall

speak later, seems so different from the traditional approaches that it has rarely been recognized as a type of religion at all. Freud, himself the founder of a great religious sect, could typically call all traditional faiths and, by implication, all "religion" merely illusion. He was typical because those practicing the new way of thinking considered that they had put away "religion" as a childish thing when they had discarded Christian or Jewish theology and called themselves atheists or agnostics. Meanwhile, in all fields, but especially in psychology, with which we are here more directly concerned, researchers developed vocabularies and criteria of thinking that made a return to the data of religion increasingly difficult, and a person trained in religion has come to sound amateurish when he tries to use the language of psychology.

The fault has by no means been all on one side. During the past forty years, the leaders of Christianity have increasingly fought back by proclaiming that man's ways of thinking and data are to be sharply divided between the sacred and the profane, the revealed and the humanly discovered. The gap has so widened that, in a conference on the subject a few years ago, I heard it generally agreed among the theologians that the data of psychology have no relevance for theology and ritual.

On the contrary, religion of one sort or another is one of the two or three universal and basic aspects of human life. As for its relation to psychology, religion has been the psychotherapy of the ages, and no one would dispute that at least what other people call their religions have been psychological experiences. The "psychology of religion," accordingly, neglected as it now is, remains a crucial part of the study of man.

But who is competent to discuss it? The ideal person would be one who has studied all types of religious experience with sympathy and understanding and who is also a trained psychologist—even more, a creative psychologist. To appraise the great body of religious data will demand that one rethink much of psychology, as one would have to do if faced with any other large body of unconsidered data. The business of the "psychology of religion" is not to fit religious experiences into the pigeonholes of Freud or Jung or into the categories of *Gestalt* or stimulus–response or any other, but rather to see what the data of religious experiences themselves suggest. Such a psychologist with such an interest has not yet appeared.

We are left with the question: Can the study be attempted by a person trained primarily in religion who knows a little psychology? This essay makes a go (I cannot use more dignified language) at describing what a single person has seen from the point of view of the history of religion. In Chapter One, the subject has to be opened by a general discussion and definition of the term "religion," or at least of the sense in which it will be used here. In Chapter Two, I try to depict the struggle for psychological integrity —one of the most important aspects of religion—as it seems to have been going on in the lives of thoughtful men in the ancient world. Next, just as I had to define the term "religion," so in Chapter Three I outline the basis of my psychological position. With this understood, we are ready for the chief section of the study, Chapter Four, in which I describe what I have concluded are the most important types of religious experience.

Even William James, the giant and despair of us all, did not set his work in such a wide perspective. His magnificent *Varieties of Religious Experience* actually describes the varieties of Protestant experience (and not all of these), with some Catholic material in supplement. He uses the categories of Protestantism throughout; he discusses the religion of healthy-mindedness, the sick soul, conversion, and mysticism, but not a word about sacraments, legal observances, the church, or the symbols, mythological fancies, and rituals which are religion for millions of people. No Catholic, Jew, Hindu, or Moslem would have used such an outline for the subject or would feel much personal relevancy in James's brilliant descriptions. And, amazingly as James anticipated much of later psychological thinking, he still wrote at the turn of the century.

I do not know whether James would like what I have written here. But I do know that, as one of the men who brought in the new age of the "Study in Human Nature," he would want me to try what I can do.

Erwin Ramsdell Goodenough

Cambridge, Massachusetts
December 1964

Contents

THE PSYCHOLOGY OF RELIGIOUS EXPERIENCES

I

What Is Religion?

A BOOK ON LOVE, LOYALTY, OR JUSTICE would gain little but
pedantry by starting out with a concise definition of the
term. Only as we describe the various conflicting elements
associated with such words can we finally arrive at a meaning that includes their complexities, for in important matters we understand, not as we simplify, but as we can tolerate
the paradoxical. Each important factor in our lives over-
laps every other aspect of life. Even such an apparently
distinct feature as childhood runs on into our maturity, so
that no adult can be understood apart from the child still
living within him.

A colleague has told me that he had once tried to define
"poetry" in such a way that his definition would include

I

all the forms of literature to which the word had been applied. When he had finished, he said, his definition had become so broad that no one had any use for it. I strongly suspect, however, that, in taking so universal an approach, he had come to an understanding of poetry much richer and deeper, even if less clear and specific, than that of those who worked with more limited statements, for clarity is often won at the expense of comprehension.

Religion presents an outstanding example of this difficulty. Those who think they know most clearly, for disapproval or approval, what religion "is" seem to recognize least what amazingly different aspects of human life the term has legitimately indicated. We can, therefore, best approach religion by getting in mind the various experiences that men have called religion, rather than what we think should ideally be given the name.

To most people, a man is religious or not according as he assents to, belongs to, follows the practices of an organized or traditional faith. When we speak of the religions of the world, we are ordinarily taken to refer to Christianity, Judaism, Islam, Buddhism, and the like. "Primitive religions," those traditionally practiced in the Pacific Islands and Central Africa or by the Australian aborigines, seem to most people to be incipient, nascent religions and not yet what can acceptably be called religion. In lectures on religion, such phenomena are usually discussed under "The Origins of Religion," as contrasted to expositions of "The World's Great Religions." The religious practices of savages are shot so full of what most people call "magic," "superstition," or "idolatry" as to seem not to have reached the level of "religion" at all. Even William James does not include religion on this level among his "varieties" of religious experience. Here I need point out only that, little as we may approve the religious ideas and practices of savages,

2

we can hardly deny that these constitute their religion. Metaphysicians and theologians usually distinguish between what seem to them to be aberrations in religion, which they do not like to call religion, and real religion, which is their own ideal formulation.

One who has studied the history of religion or anthropology must take another path, for he sees that religion lies in the act of acceptance, compliance, belief; that it is the attitude of trust, not the object trusted, which constitutes religion. When we begin to distinguish between "true" and "false" religion, we at once lose ourselves in subjectivism. The common approach to religion received its classical expression in the mouth of the Reverend Mr. Thwackum, tutor of Tom Jones: "When I mention religion I mean the Christian religion; and not only the Christian religion but the Protestant religion; and not only the Protestant religion but the Church of England."

In the end, of course, we shall all come out with judgments that are largely subjective. I shall not try to deceive my readers or myself by representing that my preferences "in no way affect my mental processes en route," as a Catholic priest once said to me about his commitment to end his researches by affirming the teachings of the Church. The religion of many people includes observances and beliefs which we may not want to make our own; but, even so, we must still agree that they fully belong in a discussion of the nature of religion as men practice it.

If religion in all its manifestations is to have any meaning for us collectively, then we must consciously or unconsciously recognize a common element in these manifestations. The common element is that of a devotion to something on which the people committed seem to themselves to depend, or in which they hope for security, or in which they actually find it. Whether it is the security given by a fetish, by a ritual, by a creed, by the church, by the loving Jesus, by one's social status, by a substantial bank account, by a title (whether the title be "president of the bank," "professor," or "marquis"), or by creativity in art or science, when one or more of these becomes the focus of our lives, we have accepted that security as our religion. Some of these are the security of humility, others are that of successful aggression; I speak of them all, for the moment, simply as sources of security.

We normally have more than one source of security. When Jesus said that we "cannot worship God and Mammon," that is, money or social power, he showed by contrast that most men, including his own followers, are actually polytheists in spite of their profession of monotheism, since most of us really do find our security, trust, in both. By our real, not our verbal, dedications are our religious characters manifest. Anything becomes a god to us as soon as we give it unquestioned devotion, whether we call it "god" or not.

Man lives now, as he has always lived, in a universe, in a human society, and with inner conflicts, all of which threaten to engulf him and some of which sooner or later certainly will do so. In helplessness people of all civilizations begin their lives and in helplessness end them. Although as adults we can somewhat fend for ourselves, all the deeper experiences of personal life and the exigencies of society emphasize the essential impotence of the individual. The mass of men in Canada, the United States, and Western Europe live in a security which other men have rarely known. That we make even of this an "age of anxiety" shows how inescapably man feels the uncertainty of life. During the "golden age" of the nineteenth century, as nostalgic cowards now often conceive it, life expectancy was just half that of our day; pain expectancy, physical

agony, cold in winter and inescapable heat in summer—
these sat with every man at his fireside and table.

I am writing at the moment in Nantucket, surrounded by
the great old whalers' mansions of a century or two ago.
The "widow's walks" atop each house, however, betray
the mental anguish of those who lived there because of the
desperate chances the men were taking to make their for-
tunes. The old Islanders of Nantucket were continuing the
life of primitive hunters, who went out with clubs and
stones to get food for themselves and their families.

The terrors of disease, of course, have always been with
all men, to disable them, torture them with pain, and finally
kill them. When men settled from hunting into farming, they
only found new terrors—those of uncontrolled weather and
of their fellowmen's desire to kill them (or later to cheat
them) in order to appropriate the cultivated ground. And
they had to face the greed of the more successfully preda-
tory, who soon became the great lords and who would
force the farmers to contribute the best of their returns
from the land so that the lord might live in a palace and,
in turn, war with other lords for the security and glory of
still greater holdings. Amos' scorching rebuke of the nobles
of Israel for their oppression of the poor was echoed in
Greek terms by Hesiod and Solon in Athens and could have
been repeated in almost every region where men lived at
any time. The French Revolution, the American Constitu-
tion, and the slow beginnings of social reform throughout
the modern world have given new financial security to the
ordinary man; modern medicine has given him greater physical security.

Yet, with all this greater security, man does not feel more
secure, because he has more time to reflect, to pity himself
for his still essential helplessness, and to write and read
about it. He torments himself afresh with the perennial

5

dream of a vanished golden age, a sort of Eden from which we have excluded ourselves by our sins. That the speed of travel now makes it possible for bad young men and boys to commit greater crimes and complicates the problem of catching them is oddly taken to indicate that the young are now more vicious than in generations past. In the "death urge," Freud did indeed point out an amazing aspect of human nature; it is an urge to kill which at one time we turned daily against animals and one another, but now turn inwardly against ourselves as we heap all sorts of fancied or possible dangers and tragedies upon those which life actually presents to us. What we used to call the "balance of power," for example, we now call the "cold war" and do so, as far as I can see, only to torture ourselves.

What I am trying to point out is that release from anxiety about one thing only allows our attention to turn to other sources of anxiety. In all directions, in nature, society, and within ourselves, we actually face threats that are more than threats, for soon each of us will perish. Since man has in addition the mental power to anticipate coming agonies and death, man is inherently an anxious animal, ever crossing fancied bridges of difficulty when no actual problems confront him. We are all cowards who "die a thousand times."

I call these threats or sense of threats collectively the "tremendum," a Latin word which Rudolph Otto used in a somewhat different sense and which has, as I use it, its simple original meaning of "that which must be feared" or "the source of terror." I use it precisely because its strange vagueness best conveys the most terrifying part of our predicament, the very inchoateness of the terror without and within us.

Human beings have generally never been able to face the terror as such. Two ineluctable necessities have always forced themselves on man. First, he cannot endure his ignorance: he must feel that in some measure he understands himself, his origin, his natural environment, and his destiny. And, second, he cannot endure his helplessness: he must give himself the illusion that he has at least a little control over things. There must be something he can do about it all. Insofar as man has the second illusion, that he can control the uncontrollable, he loses his sense of futility. The drive for control has not only produced the gadgets of civilization; it has expressed itself in religious practices of all sorts, from what higher civilizations call "magic" to the ritualistic acts and prayers of church or party and to the private rituals we all consciously or unconsciously observe. This begins with the earliest childhood: thumb-sucking, the fetishistic blanket, familiar routine in familiar surroundings —these the child early demands. He may give up some, but as he does so he will cling all the more earnestly to others. Man's rituals make the individual participate in the tremendum to a slight extent, at least, and give him a feeling that by these acts he appeases the tremendum or makes it more apt to befriend him. By the rituals he also keeps himself from consciously facing the tremendum's unfathomable depth and power, the actual abyss of the uncontrollable. We all invent little rituals, but few individuals have been able to invent enough of them to satisfy themselves. In childhood, the mother or nurse supplies them to the child. She keeps the child near her or puts him in a playpen where a fine little world is nicely boxed in for him and the universe excluded. An eighteen-month-old child is far happier in such a pen than alone in a five-acre lot. He may toddle away and get lost, but, when he finds himself really alone and cut off from the familiar, the safe, he goes to pieces. In later years, social and ecclesiastical tradition steps in with rituals and limitations.

I shall return to the religious value of law. Here I speak

of the rituals that societies have supplied in their traditions, such as those for the sick. Men have tried to cure the sick by masked dances; by special prayers; or, as some in the Church of England advocate, by using the Eucharist as a healing agent. That these, including the masked dancers, all have healing value no one—at least not I—will deny. If their power consists only in quieting the affected one, raising his morale, and hence increasing his resistance to disease and his will to survive, still their value is real. If I may generalize from history and anthropology, man loses his power to survive when he is faced with the utterly uncontrollable tremendum. We fight off reabsorption into it only as we act against it under the illusion of control.

Man throws curtains between himself and the tremendum, and on them he projects accounts of how the world came into existence, pictures of divine or superhuman forces or beings that control the universe and us, as well as codes of ethics, behavior, and ritual which will bring him favor instead of catastrophe. So has man everywhere protected himself by religion.

At this point, those who know the great religions of the East, typically Hinduism and Buddhism, will protest that what I have been saying does not apply to devotees of those religions at all. Their great ideal and hope is that the tremendum, whether they call it Brahma or Nirvana, will engulf them and extinguish their individuality—precisely what the curtains are designed to prevent. The same idea has appeared also, of course, in the great mystics of the West, and we shall come to that phenomenon later. The protest has much justification. Here is, indeed, a pattern which differs from the usual patterns of man's religion, just as Freud's death instinct contrasts with his libido and id. That instinct puzzled Freud—a thorough Westerner—and he and his followers now accepted it, now rejected it. In the Eastern craving for reabsorption, however, we see the individual death instinct plainly enough. It reappears somewhat in all religions which solve men's problems by asking of them resignation, acceptance, submission; but these manifestations are usually submission to a pattern (to a ritual, discipline, church, or higher Person), rather than to the end of the path of negation, where we disappear in the Not-So.

The contrast between religions that protect us from the tremendum by the curtains as over against religions that lead us out into personal annihilation in the tremendum will be felt chiefly by scholars who know the Eastern religions primarily from reading the religious classics. The great concern of the Eastern masses at the temples, on the contrary, is to make offerings and say prayers which will store up merit for the individual, so that in the next incarnation he will at least hold his own and not reappear in a more degraded form. A genuine craving for reabsorption does seem present in the contemplation of Buddhist monks or Hindu holy men, where the monk yields to the tremendum and tries to lose his identity as an individual in it. I am not a student of these religions, but I dare say from what I have seen and heard that very few even of these monks have any idea that they are at the final stage and will return to Nirvana at death. Rather, they devote themselves to religious exercises which, however foreign to most Western taste, really prepare them also for a better and higher reincarnation. That is, the mystic exercises in which they descend or rise into the unparticularized universal are their way of controlling that uncontrollable universe, of keeping it from actually debasing and ruining them. We may accordingly return to discussing religion in terms of its common function of protecting the individual from the tremendum by the illusion of control.

An interesting story came out of World War II. A Navy

petty officer kept his subordinates alive for weeks in an open lifeboat in the Pacific by enforcing military discipline every second. The collecting and rationing of rain water, the catching of fish and eating their vital organs for vitamins—all this went on by strict command. When the five men at last reached an island, not knowing whether friend or enemy held it, they marched up on the beach, naked but in military step, to meet what was before them. They found friends and were saved, but what had kept them going in the staggering tremendum of the Pacific was the military playpen in which their commander enclosed them. I trust that no reader will suppose I have not the greatest respect for the value of playpens for human survival.

When we have complete faith in our rituals, they tend to become acts effective by the very act, a literal translation of the Church's phrase, *ex opere operato*. If the Catholic Church can thus speak of an act's accomplishing its ends, whether by faith or by the power inherent in its officials, clearly we must abandon the usual contrast between magic and religion. Scholars like to contrast magic with religion. Magic, it is usually said, claims an actual operative power for its acts, such power that God or the demons or whatever are compelled to make the spell work, to accomplish the deed called for by the magician. The classic instance is the power Aladdin exercised through rubbing his lamp. In contrast, it is claimed, truly religious prayers only make petitions to a God wiser than men, and the truly devout bow in acceptance when God in his wisdom does not grant the petition. However much Jesus may have exemplified this attitude at Gethsemane, he is reported to have taught his disciples quite another view of prayer. It began, according to the report, when he put what would ordinarily be called a hex on a fig tree, so that it withered in a few hours.

This, he said, was only a single example of what prayer with faith can do. You can tell a mountain to rise and cast itself into the sea and it will do so, he said: indeed, anything whatever you ask in faith will happen. The one thing needful is faith. We have clearly gone utterly beyond "petition." Prayer with faith inevitably accomplishes its ends, even to tossing mountains about.

I was reading the other day about a little girl who tried it out on a mountain in her vicinity and gave up her belief in God when the mountain did not disappear. The simple fact is that, whether we try to break a drought by using incantations and wet twigs or by having the bishop include a petition for rain in cathedral ritual, in either case we do it in the belief that it is more likely to rain if we do than if we do not. In each case, the attempt is to control the otherwise-uncontrollable. People who make either approach know very well that rain does not always follow their rituals. As Knute Rockne, the famous football coach of Notre Dame, used to say: "The prayers work better when the players are big." But, however big, we still hope that saying the prayer will increase the players' powers.

I doubt that Jesus ever withered a healthy tree in a few hours by cursing it, just as I doubt that there is a magic in faith so powerful that it can move mountains or accomplish *everything* else we may desire. But I see no reason to doubt that Jesus himself honestly taught this. And I certainly see no reason for blinding ourselves to the fact that, whether in Catholic sacraments or Protestant conversions, Christianity has accomplished what from ordinary points of view seem to be miracles and given men formulas for accomplishing them. When the Protestant evangelist tells a sinner that Christ will save him and make him a new creature if he has faith, he is giving the sinner a formula, one which has actually accomplished millions of psychological miracles in clearing up and giving control of the chaotic tremendum in men's souls.

"Magic" is so powerful among savages and among a large part of our own population precisely because people have implicit faith in it. My former colleague Ralph Linton told me about a case he knew of a young Negro who came into a hospital in New York begging for help because he had been hexed and would die at noon the next day. Linton tried to convince the doctors that the man would indeed die if they did not find the person who had cast the spell and get him to relieve the man's mind. The doctors, however, merely examined the patient, found him healthy in every way, smiled at one another behind Linton's back, and put the patient to bed as a disturbed man who needed quiet. But, at noon the next day, he died, and an autopsy found nothing wrong. Now, I do not believe that the spell killed him, but I have no doubt that his belief in the power of the spell did so.

Witch doctors also cure patients, as do practitioners of faith healing. When the psychoanalysts say that they can do nothing for a patient until his "resistance" breaks down, I suspect that they have only invented a new term for the old phenomenon. They, too, can do their work only in an atmosphere of faith.

The magic of faith—is it religion or magic? The question has broken down into tautology. Faith that we can do the superhuman, such as killing or healing another person by suggestion, gives us power to do what is beyond ordinary human powers. Through faith we do control the uncontrollable—some of it, a little. Where there is faith, there is religion. Not intellectual assent but faith, deep emotional acceptance, makes a Catholic or a Voodooist. Those who have "lost their faith" often speak of the loss as though they had lost their sight or hearing, a faculty of some sort that made them able to do things to themselves and for themselves which they cannot now do. They are quite right; they have lost a real potency, a real power of control. So I must say that, to call a belief "superstition," a ritual "magic," is only to pronounce a value judgment. These are religious beliefs and acts which the person calling them "superstition" or "magic" does not like. In calling them so, we are back with Mr. Thwackum, limiting "religion" to what we ourselves approve.

As we go on to discuss in more detail the forms religion may take, we shall find many ways in which man tries to control the uncontrollable. Before leaving the subject in general, however, we must ask how this differs from man's ingenuity in inventing devices by which he indeed gives himself superhuman power—devices which range from stone implements that multiply his striking force to the airplane, atomic bomb, and computer. At the end, we shall suggest that concern with expanding knowledge can itself become a religion for scientists, but that, in general, control through understanding the forces of nature stands in sharp contrast to traditional religion, which has been an attempt to control without such understanding. If a Tyrolean peasant protects his house by building a shrine to the Virgin into its walls, we call it religion, but not when men in the Western prairies, with their terrible thunderstorms, protect their houses by putting lightning rods on them. We have a religious situation when, after Philip had converted the eunuch, as told in Acts, 8:26-40, "the Spirit of the Lord caught away Philip, and the eunuch saw him no more." If Philip had got into a helicopter and vanished almost as quickly, it would not be religion, because men understand helicopters. The contrast can be seen again in an experience of a friend of mine, a physician in Texas, who was called to help a woman with a hemorrhage. He did what he could while her adolescent son, on his knees at the foot of the bed, kept up a loud and incessant chant: "Oh Lord, we knows doctors ain't no good." Neoorthodox detractors of modern science seem to me to be carrying on the boy's chant. I notice, however, that, when ill, they call the best doctors they can find.

The present fear aroused by man's enormously increasing scientific control actually rests on the conviction that the new techniques may make man less aware of his still essential helplessness and blind him to his limitations and constant need for the traditional approaches of faith. People making this protest are right. The modern man much resembles an adolescent driver of an automobile, so elated by the new power he controls that he is often a threat to himself and others. Unless we always bear in mind the limits of our control, the tremendum does indeed often step in and, in the case of the adolescent driver, leave the boy's parents with religion as the only solace. Our new powers of scientific control have by no means put an end to invasions of the uncontrollable tremendum. I cannot assert that men will never be able entirely to control the tremendum for their own ends, but I can say that even adequate control does not now appear even remotely possible. Such control might do away with man's need of religion, at least as we have mostly understood religion, but we do not have to discuss that eventuality seriously. Man has always been, is now, and apparently ever will be in need of feeling the sort of control he has always felt through faith in religious acts, objects, and beliefs. We shall see that these faiths enter by the back door, like the expelled demons of Jesus' parable, when we discard the old faiths.

I have just referred to the second universal in man's religious pattern in speaking of man's "beliefs." By this I do not mean his control through scientific knowledge, but the creeds, myths, and philosophical and theological systems by which he gives himself the illusion that he understands the tremendum. Perhaps we will some day know better, but, as far as we can now see, man alone has this craving to understand. Some people, of course, have the craving more than others, but all people of normal intelligence have to have a sense that they understand nature and their place in it or that their leaders or priests do so. In ancient days, and still among savages, the authorities are usually the "old men." These sages created stories or, more usually, passed on stories which they had heard in turn from their seniors in an indefinite succession of old men—stories of creation, of the origins of evil and the necessity for work, of the stars, the heavens, the depths of the sea, of the origins of life and death, of male and female, good and evil, and of life after death. Such stories the old men told in personal form, as though in answer to the questions of four- and five-year-old children: "Who made the world?" "Where is Grandma, who died?" "Who makes the thunder?" "Who blows the wind?" "Who paints the grass green?" "Who makes the waves in the sea?" The answers we give our children are also apt to be personal, in terms of God the Creator. But in primitive times almost all answers were centered in persons, so that all nature became populated with personalities, most of them greater and more powerful than man, but in other respects quite like him. Other such "persons" had the spooky character of the forms men meet in dreams—phantoms, yet with human personalities and motives.

The advance of science has put such abstractions as law, gravity, and electric power in the place of most of these personalities, but nonscientific civilizations still account for the storms and plagues as manifestations of the wrath of divine persons, much as Homer did. Insanity and illness are seen as demonic possession. Man can face the perils of life so much better if he believes that he understands or that the medicine man understands. If Christianity and science have since given us different sorts of answers, the primitive still survives in most families in the form of what we call "old wives' tales." Almost universally we resort to the primitive in the face of catastrophe. One of the constant problems in dealing with the parents of a defective child is to take from them the sense that God has marred the child to punish the parents for some sins they have committed. If a tragedy happens, a Person has done it. The idea even has current legal status in what the law describes as "acts of God"—all disasters from such natural causes as storms or floods.

We ordinarily call mythology the attempt to explain nature in terms of such personalities and their attitudes. But, if we now define a myth as an explanation given to conceal from ourselves our lack of understanding, then myths are with us in all modern life. Like most people, I am not a natural scientist, and so the scientific accounts as I finally understand them and the implications I draw of how the forces of nature operate are all ridiculously mythological from the point of view of pure science. I accept with utter credulity the latest theories of medicine, nervous energy, the origin and organization of the universe—which are these same primitive questions in abstract form. I am neither a vitalist nor a nonvitalist because scientists themselves do not agree on the subject, but am ready to go either way when they decide, whether I myself understand them or not. Meanwhile, of course, I live in a mythical world in which "dead" and "alive" are absolute opposites, and I find for my purposes that that myth serves very well. I use my pseudo-scientific myths of nature for two reasons: first, to have a rough and ready understanding with which I can meet the problems of life and, second, to have a sense that I am not lost and helpless in a meaningless tremendum. And, as we shall see, my structure as a parent, moral person, and citizen is based entirely on myths of "right"and "wrong." Ancient myths and creeds served all these purposes.

Individuals have rarely dared to face the fact that they live in an unknown world, about them and within, and no society has tried to face it. "Agnosticism" is an unpopular word, and agnostics are suspect individuals because they challenge the presence of man's beliefs and throw men back on their ignorance and helplessness, which, by their myths and rituals, they are trying to conceal from their own horrified eyes. To live in awareness of their ignorance would crush the vast majority of human spirits. So between themselves and the incomprehensible-uncontrollable they have dropped curtains and projected upon them their myths, codes, rites, and beliefs to give themselves the illusion that they understand the nature of the universe and how to control it and themselves in it for their benefit and security.

The projected God or gods, stories of creation and afterlife, rules of ethics, rituals of expiation and appeasement help as they become vivid like dreams, become actual to us through faith. The designs or codes we thus project upon the curtains fulfill, like dreams, our desires, but unlike dreams they become permanently stamped or painted on the curtains in which we wrap ourselves. In dreams, we project fleeting cinemas of wish-fulfilling symbolism. In religion, the projections become fixed, painted on the curtains, the designs so fixed, indeed, the curtains so firmly woven that we can pass them on to our children as we "bring them up in the faith" or "indoctrinate" them. Whole civilizations may be so oriented to them that they are ready to kill those who challenge their claim to represent the nature of the tremendum adequately.

In this way, we get the secure illusion that we live, not in the universe of natural forces which are as far from pity as a tornado or bolt of lightning, but in a universe ruled by love or kindness or by a God who has special favors for our selves, our sect, or our people, however he may blast the others. We ourselves need not face the vasty deep of the tremendum.

Scholars have taken such notions as *mana* or "the idea of the holy" in contrast to the profane to be the basis of mankind's religious life. But none of them prove to be universal, and each has been challenged by other scholars. They are themselves specific, if widely found, patterns for curtains. The common element is no one design, but the insecurity and universal anxiety which various peoples and individuals all experience, along with the equally universal craving for explanation and control which prompts them everywhere to project or repeat primitive or elaborate myths, rites, creeds, and faiths, to make painted curtains about them. The vast majority of men get these curtains and their designs ready-made from their societies, whether from dogmas given by professional religious groups; from the "old men" or "old women" of the tribe; or, often today, from party leaders, journalistic reports, or college courses that introduce us to the fringes of scientific theory and give us the illusion of understanding. Religion accepts such stories as truths, not hypotheses, and makes men pattern their lives on them. Not the truth of an account, but its basic acceptance as truth and one's commitment to it, constitutes religion. True or false, the stories become the basis of our religion when they are accepted as describing our universe, the reality in which we live, and when they actually make the unformed tremendum seem something we can consider formed and manageable.

I write this in humility, for I know myself as a religious

man. In very few aspects of my own life do I really have evidence for the validity of what I am living by. Yet my life would indeed have been chaos if I had not taken certain "truths to be self-evident," beginning with the very dubious truths announced by that phrase of the Declaration of Independence. In writing this book, I am myself painting a curtain. Insofar as any man lives by the ideas and conceptions which give his life meaning, he is living within a painted curtain, is being religious. Life has meaning only as we give it meaning. Accordingly, all men are religious, whether in the illusory terms of a traditional creed or code, in the equally illusory conception of the Enlightenment that man is a rational being who can live by reason, in the world of Mammon, or some other. For all men must live by a set of values, however unconsciously and however the values may contradict one another. That is why religion is universal in history and anthropology and must be so.

A design of social standards on our curtains, one by which we distinguish right from wrong, is equally essential. We cannot exist without society, and no society can endure without a definite scheme of what it permits and forbids. Each tribe must adjust to life within a given natural environment, must offer security within the tribe, must have a clear understanding of the family and of permitted sexual relations, and must have a workable idea of property. The tribe also early develops a police power to see that the individual members do nothing that will displease the gods or, in more general terms, bring misfortune from the anger of the divine forces as understood in terms of the tribe's painted curtains. What one tribe or civilization considers right often so contradicts the beliefs of other tribes that scholars have long considered ethics "relative." The term shocks conservative believers of all civilizations because on the curtains of each is written what they take to be the inherently, even metaphysically, correct practices for living. These standards of conduct have always been part of the "religion" of the group, and in many civilizations they formed the essential core of religion.

The drama of the Greeks expressed deep conviction that the gods and fates ultimately set and sanctioned the basic laws of men, so much so that the unwitting offenses of Oedipus had to be punished as definitely as though he had offended with intent, and the long chain of agonized sanctions of the *Oresteia* could be broken only by the direct interference of Athena herself. The laws imposed by the Greek gods seem at first quite unlike those promulgated by Yahweh or Mohammed or those which Christians believe to be the standard at the Last Judgment. We will all agree that at least the Greek gods and their standards are mythological. They are designs slowly painted on the curtains over millennia of experience by the ancestors of Greek civilization, worked out, presumably, in response to the social and psychological needs of successive civilizations.

My point is that man's conduct and the legal structure of his society, man's sense of right and wrong, play as deep a part in man's religious structure as his cosmogonic myths and ritual requirements for worship. Men cannot live without some sense of right, and every society must have a sense of the rightness of its own customs. An individual may break off, call himself amoral, or feel himself as completely independent of ordinary social rules as did the Greek tyrants whom the Sophists defended—or as did Hitler. But people can do this only when they can convince themselves that popular notions of right are really wrong, at least for the more energetic and capable spirits, and that they do a higher right in flouting them. Hitler's passionate self-righteousness was his most compelling asset, and the same was true of Khrushchev. That is, if a man rejects the ethical myths his society has painted for him on the curtains he must paint new ones for himself and believe them, since the survival of either a society or an individual requires a firm belief that the system by which it or he lives is right. We may suffer guilt as a divided soul, but some part of us must feel we are doing as we should. We can always justify a traditional myth by saying that it has served its purpose of adjusting men to nature and to other members of society, has made it possible for them to live consecutively and productively, and that there must therefore be some truth behind its claim to be right.

Today, many of the intelligentsia have lost the old patterns, and the loss has deeply affected, not only their "religion," but the thinking and stability of many of our politicians and international lawyers, who find that they had been getting security from a myth-covered curtain all along. Our political reactionaries are simply cowards who cling to the old projected securities to avoid facing reality.

We must all agree, however, that in law tradition as such has great value. Except for a few philosophic minded lawyers, the courts have always operated by their own unchallenged codes. Personally, lawyers are as free as anyone else to consider religious and ethical problems critically, but in drawing up briefs to demonstrate what should be decided in court they deal with as absolute a body of "right" as any orthodox Jew or Catholic. To them, precedent—the law as established by legislatures and interpreted by courts —has, even in courts of equity, final validity, so that lawyers have long and often spoken of the "sanctity" of the law. True, when lawyers follow the precedents and forms of legal tradition too closely, they often create injustice and connive with mere craftiness. The situation disturbs our most thoughtful attorneys, but it does not unsettle their confidence, which I by no means dispute, that the orderly operation of a nation's traditional code is itself right.

How much of all this legal formulation of the right should we call religion? Certainly there is no debate that in primitive times *all* of it was religion, as it still is in savage societies. In orthodox Judaism from the earliest Israelitic times to the present, no one has disputed that, whether the individual obeyed or not, religion was primarily a set of rules for all of life. Even today, after the centuries in which lawyers and rulers have tried to free law and government from their former "religious" ties of the Middle Ages, our law courts are still conducted in an atmosphere of religious pageantry. The judges are robed and addressed with titles that set them apart from ordinary men; the witnesses are compelled to invoke God to attest their truthfulness. "Contempt of court" bears every resemblance to impiety or sacrilege. The crier in the Supreme Court in calling to order ends "God bless the United States and this honorable court." All this is part of the painted curtain with which society must surround its courts to survive, for thereby society can pretend to itself that its legal routine is really that of the tremendum and keep the actual tremendum from disrupting it.

What we call the secularizing of law and the state has only meant freeing them from the control of organized ecclesiastics. Those who in our own past wished to secularize law never wanted to divorce society and its ethics or law or regimentation finally from the idea of the holy or sacred. They simply hoped to free the practices and ideas of law from control by priests. Like all religious organization, the state and its structure depend upon being devoutly accepted by the populace. Whether the state and its laws should get the quality of divinity through a church or through its own "sanctity" as a bulwark between men and the chaos of the tremendum, that is, through "popular sovereignty," can be violently disputed, as it has been; but we do not dispute that the tribe or state must in the end have a sanctity that can command man's devotion to the death, as well as through life. In a democracy, whether so formally stated or not, the "voice of the people" must be the "voice of God" or there can be no state. And this is religion.

Can modern men go on with an adequate sense of the rightness of their way of life while admitting the full and equal right of others to have a totally different way? When Russians and Americans meet or, rather, when the rulers of both meet as high priests of differing "ways," the deepest danger is from religious bigotry on both sides. A war between the Soviet Union and the United States would be a religious war, as, indeed, were both the great wars of this century. In those wars, both sides believed that defeat would mean, not simply military and material humiliation, but the tearing of all their curtains and a complete inundation of the tremendum. The chaos in Germany after World War I was so devastating that most Germans were delighted to have a curtain bearing even the picture of Hitler rather than no curtain at all, though it meant the gas chambers and firing squads as his altars and ritual.

In seeing how basically religion is used to protect us from the tremendum in problems of society, we see that, in law and politics, what protects is a sense that we know the right, that we can explain the inexplicable ultimate of human relations. Our public schools are organized to teach democracy as a final faith, and few among even private schools and universities dare keep as teachers people who want even to discuss this as an open question. The Russians, similarly, have no place for a man who doubts the final truth of their conceptions of society. No state can succeed without such a religious foundation.

. . .

If, in our relations with both nature and society, we have faced the tremendum by creating within ourselves an illusion that we understand it, we must face the other tremendum, the one within us, in the same way. We know actually even less about this inner world than about the world of nature and society, for we have no way at all to observe the inner world directly. The "censor" within us represses our doubts, our sense of ignorance about ourselves and about how we should regulate our private lives, and gives us the illusion that we know how we should live and act, know what our own desires and motives really are. Except for actual psychotics, the great mass of men seem to have followed codes which the inner control, the censor, had relatively little trouble in enforcing.

In Christian countries, dichotomies certainly exist, as they always have, between teachings about love, honesty, and justice, on the one hand, and man's actual practices, on the other. But the practices were those really, if tacitly, sanctioned by society, and the Church eased her burden of idealism by offering absolution for offenses against her ideal code. Or, as among the old British colonial administration in India and still in South Africa and Protestant America, in matters of business and race relations the churches have condoned a double standard by helping us conceal from ourselves that we had one. During the past sixty years, we have discovered the subjective tremendum in the unconscious, the fixation of our patterns in childhood, the dubiety and inconsistency of our motives. The discovery has for the first time made general the sense of guilt which always haunted religious geniuses—the Buddha, Amos, Paul, Augustine, Luther, Gandhi, and millions of lesser men.

Psychiatry and depth psychology have thrown the book at us. They create guilt in us without offering a superhuman salvation, create it by making us aware of the mixed character of our motives, of our inner revolt against what society has taught us to call "good." We shall see that this problem of guilt is by no means a new one. But traditional religion handled it by atoning sacrifices and sacraments, by religious exercises of penance, prayer, and forgiveness, or by vivid gifts of God's grace. I was brought up to consider myself morally a "worm," but comforted by the conviction that the Prince of Glory "had devoted his sacred head for such a worm as I." Modern analysis offers only the many-thousand-dollar couch, where results are little more successful, qualitatively or numerically, than were those of the mourners' bench. The problems of humanity will not be solved, however, one by one on those couches.

We now know that hate is the normal concomitant and reverse side of love and see it in ourselves. The value of games for children in expressing this side of their nature has freshly appeared to us; but we know that, in the bitter competitions of life, in our cruelty to our subordinates and children by which we avenge the cruelty we suffered from our parents and still suffer from those "above" us or the more "successful," in all this we now recognize a vital and original sin which baptism and penance do not affect in the slightest and which we are too self-conscious to cure by conversion. And we are all frightened at the new outlets man now has for expressing his destructive nature. Just at the time when man more than ever needs the help of an illusion that he really knows right from wrong in the world at large and that he can control his conduct and sanity by reference to it, we seem to have discovered the real meaning of original sin within our divided selves, as well as the fictitious character of the patterns by which we formerly pulled ourselves together. To modern man, original sin has become man's double-mindedness, that is, the fact that love implies hate, so that our motives can never become "pure" and so that we are most cruel to those we love.

We have indeed destroyed much of the old peace of mind, done so because we know that the old understanding of man and how he lives was an almost complete misunderstanding. We offer our children less clearly cut models to incorporate into their psychic structures, that is, less sharply drawn paintings for the censors within them to enforce. The younger generation reflects this in its naturally picking up our negatives and dubieties, for these actual gaps in our curtains affect our children more powerfully than our verbal assertions of moral convictions and standards of value. These youngsters who can take it seem to me to be coming into a maturity, an ability to live their own lives, to construct their own standards, which the young of my generation much more rarely had, though on this I have no statistics.

For its new awareness of the inner tremendum, the modern world pays a terrific price in the wastage of neurotics, delinquents, beatniks, and other victims of and capitalizers on noncomformity—people who feel that they have nothing to which they should conform. The Catholic Church has the answer if we want order and control at any intellectual price, but, for those who share in the growing knowledge of man's psychology, the order it offers has become the neat order of crosses on the battlefields of the past. Catholic, Protestant, and Jewish leaders offer us "peace of mind," which only the intellectually dead can accept. We may have such ordered peace of mind only as we retire to the quiet past, that is, as the modern sense of ignorance and search dies within us and we no longer struggle for the new knowledge. Perhaps we do struggle in architecture or physics or even as textual critics of the Bible, but, if we retire from our studies to houses still curtained with the old

patterns, part of us has atrophied. Until we have more objective understanding of human nature, we can paint only
subjective and uncontrolled designs, practical expediencies,
on our curtains, and these, however we live by them, can
give us no settled peace. But, as we see the traditional designs fading from our curtains in spite of the conservatives,
we become poignantly aware of how profoundly religion
has in the past contributed to life—life in ourselves as well
as in society and in relation to the universe.

Thus far I have been trying to clarify some of the implications of the term "religion." We have found that it is
basically man's adjustment to the tremendum. Before the
age of science, an adjustment was made partly through
happy empirical discoveries, such as clothing and fire; the
healing efficacy of certain plants; and the possibility of do-
mesticating certain animals and crops. That list could go on
indefinitely, but it is based not so much on man's trying to
understand the forces of nature as on his noticing that one
thing worked better than another. Religion began with
man's trying to go beyond this empirical knowledge to an
over-all rationale for his universe, his fellows, and himself,
to get means to control the empirically uncontrollable. He
has done this, I have tried to show, first, by projecting his
desires and fancies, by imagining that these or those forces
or personalities, usually many of them, control what happens and, second, by hoping that by doing the "right" thing
in ritual or social conduct these forces would be propitiated
and make his lot more pleasant now and in a future life.

I must warn the reader that I shall at the end recommend
that he still have the courage to continue to do something
much like this, even though he recognizes what religion has
always been, but to do so with awareness, since the new psychological awareness is beginning to force itself on us. What-

ever be the end, we cannot now revive the eighteenth-century dream of rationality and scientific knowledge as the full and adequate basis of conduct. I would certainly have us use all the knowledge we have and be as reasonable and critical as possible. But we still know too little about nature, society, and our psychological structures to be able to walk, as Paul rightly despaired of doing, by sight rather than faith.

As of the present or the remotely foreseeable future, the illusion that man can live by knowledge is one of the least satisfactory projections to throw on our curtains, for we still live in ignorance of the real implications of almost everything we do. Until he is omniscient, man must live by religious trust in the patterns he projects on his curtains, which means, so far as I can see, that he will always have to live by religious faith. The problem of modern men is that they must live by the designs on their curtains even though they recognize their limitations and imperfections. We must make our lives conform to our curtains and yet at the same time regard them critically. Modern man is still the ignorant man, the timid man, the insufficient man, one who has become fully aware for the first time that his mind questions what he must live by. Modern man, with his new sense of the criteria of historical evidence, questions the historical validity of most of the claims for "revealed" documents. Our universe has grown so much beyond our understanding that it is difficult any longer to conceive of a Personality so large and great as to have created it and to be managing it. This is only part of the difficulty, for, if we recognize the inadequacy of our old faiths, it still remains that only by faith, by belief in curtains and their designs, can we come into a stability which gives life any value.

This little book is by no means written to advocate the superior merits of any one type of solution for the problem, but to show how varied have been the types of solution. In the temporary double role of historian and psychologist, my aim is to describe in which ways men have acted in this matter and still tend to act, not how they ought to live or think.

I make bold at the outset to tell how intelligent men of the ancient world tried to reconcile the conflicts within their own psyches. Their ideas on the subject are not generally known by classicists, far less so by psychologists, but their thought contributed deeply to Christian teaching and experience and seems to me to have newly reappeared in modern psychology.

2

The Divided Self in
Greco-Roman Religion

WE ORDINARILY ASSOCIATE the religion of the classical period
with the Olympian gods, state and private cults, myths,
epics, drama, art, and the like. Certainly all these have to be
considered if we discuss ancient religion as a whole. But
another variety of the religious experience of Greeks and
Romans, as we see it now, began with the Orphics and
Pythagoreans (or perhaps with the Dionysiacs, of whose
early teaching we know almost nothing) and continued
through Plato, Aristotle, the Stoics, the later Pythagoreans

and Platonists, and on into Hellenistic Judaism and early Christianity.

In this tradition, man's personality appears as essentially a unit, but made up of various parts, which are often in conflict with one another. Hence, man's most important problem is to know how to resolve his inner tensions. The Orphic form of the tradition—the earliest which we can with any probability reconstruct—taught that in man a bodily element, itself the base of strong compulsions, had combined with a psyche, or mind, which was originally a fragment of the divine substance.

Myths to explain why such fragments had broken away from the divine source took two forms. In the first, the fragment had been guilty of some fault in heaven or wherever, so that its breaking away was an expulsion or fall. Its business was then to expiate its guilt so that it could return to the source. Plato assumes this conception in his *Phaedo*, and it lies behind the more dramatic picture of the horses and charioteer in the *Phaedrus*. In a second form of explanation, the fragment, itself innocent, had been torn away by a wicked force outside itself. This was presented in the myth of the Titans, primordial monsters who represented the evil power inherent in matter. In the story, they kidnaped a divine child and devoured him, though enough was saved so that a second divine child could be produced. By devouring the first child, the Titans had brought into matter fragments of the divine life and substance, whose business also was to struggle away from their entombment in matter to return to the source. According to this form of the story, the highest element in man is essentially guiltless, though it can be, and usually is, sullied by its contact with matter and has to fight to become pure enough to return.

In either form, the tradition dramatized in myth a tension which man feels so deeply within himself that it is central in all psychologies worthy of the name. Some people are more aware of the division than others. We may, as do I, deny the probability of any such psyche–soma dualism and believe that the mind or psyche is at bottom a bodily function. But we have by no means as yet discovered that bottom, and in fact we all must live with a practical sense that mind and body are distinct entities. Further, we are often "of two minds" on a subject. The compulsion to gratify what we call bodily or egocentric drives, in contrast to a compulsion to repress these desires for social or divine approval, is almost universally intelligible because it is almost universally felt. Sex offers an obvious example: it is a bodily impulse which creates psychological desires, but is one against many of whose gratifications society, one's "ideals," or both often protest. Indulgence of other appetites, as well as greed for money or power, can cause the same conflict with one's "higher principles." The Greek philosophers analyzed directly this sort of conflict within the human psyche.

Plato thought that the body represented itself in the psyche as a multiplicity of desires. The need for food and the discomfort without it are physical, but knowing what it is we desire is a function of intellect, as is all desire for anything specific. In recognizing that desire is a psychological experience, Plato went far indeed in psychology. The various desires might be considered individually, or they might be discussed collectively and represented together in the figure of the unruly horse in the *Phaedrus*. Here Plato describes the psyche as made up of three parts, which he compared to a charioteer trying to manage two horses. "Desire" is one of these horses, the one which gives the charioteer his greatest trouble. But this horse is always a collective symbol of the multifarious desires with which man's mind has to struggle. The second horse corresponds to the "spirited part" of the psyche, where the emotions seem to be central. The charioteer himself is the reason, or intellect, which was for Plato the Orphic fragment of divinity within him. Despite some cooperation from the "spirited" horse, the horse named "desire" is so unruly that it plunges the entire psyche from heaven into incarnation in a body. The only hope still is that somehow the charioteer, reason, will regain control so that the whole psyche can return to the upper regions where it properly belongs.

Unity in such a composite psyche, inner integration, Plato taught, is a matter of the harmonious coordination of its various parts and members, the control of desires and emotions by the intelligence. He called such harmonic adjustment *dikaiosunē*, a term from social life which ordinarily means "justice." Social justice to the Greeks consisted in giving to each man what was due him according to his rank, service, crime, or whatever. But Plato used the word to describe a subjective state also, and there it meant that, in the complexity of man's soul, each element should wholly fulfill its function, but should abide within its proper limits. All the parts should work fully and freely together to make a harmonious whole. So the Greek word for "justice" in the subjective realm meant very much what we would now call "psychological adjustment" or "integration."

This is the theme of Plato's *Republic*, wherein Plato discusses psychological justice, not social justice. Plato begins by presenting the ideal figure of the just man, then allows himself to be distracted by Sophistic definitions of justice which are indeed social. By Book II, however, he is already turning the reader's attention to the fact that justice is not essentially what happens in one's relations with other men, but is a quality within an individual person, one which finds its ends and values there. He returns to the political state only because, in the state, justice is presented in larger letters, and so he may get hints from the nature of justice in the state which may lead him to discover what justice should be in the soul. He therefore creates an imaginary state whose one claim to reality is that its social divisions correspond to what seem to him to be the threefold divisions of the soul: reason, emotion (if I may so translate *thumos*, the "spirited part"), and desire. The just state, we learn, is the state, whether social or personal, in which these three each function within their proper limits, that is, where reason, the natural king, can rise to conceive ideal truth and by it guide and control the lower members. *The Republic* ends in a myth of individual salvation which, as in the *Phaedo* and elsewhere, can come only to those who have thus subjugated their desires and emotions to reason.

In the *Symposium* and *Phaedrus* we are brought to the same conclusion in terms of the proper use of love, the conclusion that the basic task of man is to order his subjective chaos and that the way to do this is for him to get his highest part, his mind, back into relation with the world of supernal reality. Plato would have had deep objection to calling this higher world "the Infinite," but he considered it overwhelmingly superior in kind to anything to be found elsewhere. It was not only superior, but utterly different. In modern terms, the problem for Plato centered in the ordering and controlling of the libido by one's intelligent grasp of what Freud still calls, though not in the Platonic sense, "reality" as a whole.

Plato never abandoned the Socratic idea that man would inevitably try to get what seemed to him most desirable. If the passions so dominated his life that they obscured any real vision of a better way, then the man would live by his passions. But if he really saw a higher or different value which offered him greater rewards, the powers of the bodily passions would weaken, and the man would inevitably disregard them. Plato nowhere shows the slightest interest in will power. The mind is strong enough to hold back the horses (to use the figure closest to will power in Plato) according as it perceives higher values than can the horses, especially the horse which represents the bodily desires. In all of this, Plato was very close to modern psychoanalysis, at least in principle, for here, too, the cure of the distraught and libido-harassed soul is to be found in knowledge, not in exhortations to greater effort. Likewise, Plato never considered saving knowledge a matter simply of verbal instruction in ethics. Each mind must see for itself the higher reality, or it can have no power to control the passions. It must itself perceive what is really most worthy of being desired. This is still the heart of psychotherapy.

With his characteristic rejection of Platonic language, Aristotle, as usual, held to much the same position as Plato. There is for him a lower mind which speaks for the desires, works out ruses for gratifying them, and furnishes a motive power which leads to action when what seems to be best in a given situation has been determined. This lower mind in many ways resembles what is discussed now in terms of conditioned reflexes and stimulus–response, though Aristotle was more aware than stimulus–response psychologists often have seemed to be of the complications presented by such words as "imagination," "the calculating power," "thought," "mental images," and "restraint." Under the lower mind are two faculties of the soul much like those of Plato—sensation and what might be called desire, or drive. Although Aristotle by no means used these terms consistently, they suggest the range of his psychological speculation. Above the lower mind and its faculties is a mind which is the source of immediate perception of truth, as well as of all the distinctive processes of theoretical reasoning. Aristotle was not consistent on the matter, but it is dubious that he considered the higher mind to be a part of one's own person. All the other functions of one's soul are apparently inalienable parts of the physical organism inseparable from it and destined to perish with it. Aristotle wrote:

> As to the [higher] mind and the speculative power, . . . it seems likely that it is a distinct kind of soul, and that it alone [of the kinds or parts of the soul within us] can be separated after the analogy of the contrast of the eternal and the perishable. But the other parts of the soul clearly cannot be separated, as some say they can.[1]

Aristotle is purely Orphic-Platonic in this, and he agrees with Plato and Socrates in practically disregarding the will. We inevitably act when we seem to ourselves to recognize what is to our greatest advantage or what is "good" for us. Self-control was therefore to Aristotle (and I think he was entirely right) not the power arbitrarily to choose one course of action rather than another so much as it was a man's power to present to his mind, when seduced by immediate desires and values, a more remote and ultimately greater advantage. His desires would thereby be directed toward the truly "good" for him, and his actions would follow his desires. Like Plato, Aristotle was fully aware that mere acquaintance with higher principles or value systems, verbal acknowledgment of them, will by no means hold their ground in the face of strong immediate desires for pleasure. If intelligence in ethical matters implies knowing not so much what makes for health or strength or immediate

[1] *De Anima* 413ᵇ 24–29. This seems to deny at least the survival after death of such personality traits as memory, if not the survival of the personality as such at all.

pleasure as what makes for the good life,[2] by control we "preserve the intellect," keep such perceptions from being swamped by immediate gratifications.[3]

The problem is simply: Can we so strengthen and clarify our highest mind that it will at all times give us a vivid sense of the true values of life, so vivid, indeed, that the desire for higher values will steadily dominate lower and destructive desires? Aristotle therefore belongs fully to this tradition we are discussing, because he sees, first, the complications of the human personality and, second, that the good life consists in making man's highest power, his perception of the basically good (relatively basic, if not absolutely), so strong that all the conflicts of life will resolve themselves in one supreme aim and desire, the desire for the good life, at last properly understood. So would Aristotle try to achieve what Plato wanted—a harmonious adjustment of the parts of the soul.

From what little we know of Stoic psychology, the most important school after Aristotle, it is clear that the Stoics denied in theory the multiple parts of the psyche. In accordance with their materialistic pantheism, they tended to obliterate basic distinctions in order to make all things ultimately one. So they asserted the unity of the soul, taught that the soul in an individual is an immediate presence of the God-Matter in its original and purest sense. This constitutes the highest part of the soul, the reason and what should be the "guide." Chrysippus even went on to identify the personality with this central source.

In practice, however—like people today who dislike the old divisions of the soul into faculties or such recent divisions as those of Freud and Jung—the Stoic, too, had to

[2] *Eth. Nic.* 1140ᵃ 25-28.
[3] *Ibid.*, 1140ᵇ 7-17.

discuss the actual life of man, whether within himself or in relation to his material and human environment, in terms that quite contradicted such a unity of the soul. Man should live a life, the Stoic taught, in which the reason, which is the Universal or God purely present in him, completely guides his emotions and conduct. In this consists human freedom, freedom to accept all the vicissitudes of life with unemotional composure, because one recognizes the rightness, the unique rightness, of the universal principle which controls one. So do the external and internal controls become one in experience as they are one ontologically. But this implies a warfare between desire and intellect as much for the Stoic as for the Platonist, so that the Stoics in practice were as dualistic or pluralistic as any ancient school. The struggle for virtue consists very little in a struggle for "good" social conduct. The Stoics never became legalists in the sense that they spent their time disputing whether to allow this or that specific act—the sense in which I shall use the term "legalism" in a later chapter. They struggled much more with their inner emotions, with the seductions of pleasure and emotion in general, because they believed that man is good only when he acquiesces totally and quietly in the Way or Law of Nature. In this, they thought, lies man's freedom; they often said that the good man, the man thus organized within, is the only one who is free.

The Stoics hoped to attain such a state, which they called "apathy," in a typically Socratic-Platonic way. But, whereas Platonic justice meant the control of desires, their use (really in a sublimated form, as described in the *Symposium*), the Stoic apathy meant their elimination. One Stoic fragment shows how close the Stoics really came to the basic notions of Freud.

Every *pathos* [which we may perhaps translate "emotional impulse"] is compulsory, so that while those who are in the power of the impulses may see that it will be of advantage not to do a given thing, still they are carried along by the intensity of their feelings as by an unruly horse, and are induced to do it just the same. . . . And all those who are thus oriented in their emotional impulses turn themselves away from reason, not in a way comparable to those who are deceived in all respects, but they turn away from reason on peculiar or individual points. . . . When people are oriented in their emotional impulses, even if they learn and are elaborately instructed in the fact that one ought not to give way to pain or fear, or in general to live in the emotional impulses of the soul, still those people do not keep away from these things, but are led by the emotional impulses into the condition of being completely ruled by their tyranny.[4]

This was to the Stoic a "pathological"[5] condition, one of illness, as compared to the healthy state of a man who lives motivated only by his reason. "Every fool," that is, one who has not true wisdom, "is mad." Virtue and knowledge are identical, but instruction does not give such knowledge, guilty as a Stoic might feel from not obeying the precepts that his teachers had taught him. The knowledge which will really heal the sick soul is a sort of illumination, apparently, which may come upon a man when he sleeps. Even a man who advances in virtue or toward saving knowledge, is still a fool until the light suddenly bursts upon him, though his progress may be indicated, Zeno said, in his dreams. One who has finally come through is indeed a new creature.

[4] From Stobaeus *Anthologium* (ed. Wachsmuth and Hense) II.89 f. (= *Eclogues* II.vii.10ª). This may be from Zeno himself, since the fragment, which begins in this edition on p. 57, is ascribed to "Zeno and other Stoics."

[5] From meaning illness by being too emotional, the word "pathos" has come to mean illness in general, as a pathological condition of one's kidney, but in psychology the word still has its original meaning.

Since his distinctive acquisition is knowledge, or *sophia,* men properly call him the Wise Man, or *sophos.*

But the Stoics failed at the strategic point, namely, to explain how one can get this saving knowledge and so become a wise man. Plato had his ladder of love as well as his ladder of reason through the general studies up to dialectic, at the culmination of which the light of true knowledge and perception of reality might break in. But the Stoics seem in general to have been content to strive toward the ideal with little explanation of method and less hope of final success. Socrates, Zeno, and a few others might perhaps have succeeded, but if even these then a very few if any more.

For the history of religion as well as of psychology, however, the Stoic approach made several profound contributions to the common notion. Plato and Aristotle—drawing, I am sure, on Persian models—had dreamed of a philosopher-king who would lead men into a social order that would reflect metaphysical reality. But both saw that if, by a miracle, there should occasionally arise any such person, society could never count on a steady supply of them. So Plato and Aristotle both turned to constitutional government, and the saving "divine man" played little part in their thinking at the end. In Stoic thought, however, permanent value seemed to lie in the very dream that there might at one time have been a few such persons or even one. There was not in Stoicism an explicit teaching that a saving influence for others radiated from the one perfect Wise Man, but the delight which Stoics took in considering his sinless and ideal character, the way they thought that such a person would have been a special incarnation of the universal Reason, Law of Nature, or Logos, gave to the Stoic Wise Man a saving value which, if not formulated, seems to be to have been very real.

•   •   •

The great religious movement of Hellenistic Judaism and its still greater daughter, Hellenistic Christianity, although they both used all these Greek formulations of the divided soul, followed most closely another group, the Pythagoreans of the Hellenistic and Roman periods. The Pythagorean writings to which I allude survive, like most philosophic compositions of the Hellenistic period, only in fragments. It is impossible now to date the actual fragments. Since, as we shall see, Philo had quite similar views, we may assume that in general their point of view was familiar at least by the first century before Christ.

I shall content myself with a few interesting quotations from these writings. The first is from a book, *On Virtue*, ascribed to one Theages, of whom we know only the name. He begins with the threefold division of the soul familiar from Plato:

And the organization of the soul is as follows: one part of it is the reason, the second is the spirited part, and the third desire. When these three pass into one by manifesting a single attunement to one another, then virtue and concord come into being in the soul. But, when these strive and are detached from one another, then vice and the out-of-tune come into being in the soul. And, when the reason rules over the unreasoning parts of the soul, then endurance and continence come into being—endurance in the domination of pain and continence in the domination of pleasures. But, when the unreasoning parts of the soul rule over the reason, then weakness and incontinence come into being in the soul—weakness in that one flees from pains and incontinence in that one is conquered by pleasures. But, when the better part of the soul rules and the worse is ruled, and the one leads and the other follows, and each consents to and agrees with the other, then virtue and complete goodness come into being throughout the whole soul. And, when the desirous part of the soul follows the reasoning part, self-control comes into being; and, when the spirited part [follows the reasoning part], courage [comes into being]. And, when all the parts [follow the reasoning part], justice [comes into being], for it is justice which separates all the virtues and evils of the soul from one another. Justice is a sort of organization of the attunement of the parts of the soul and is virtue perfect and supreme; for all things are included under justice, and the other goods of the soul do not [exist] apart from it. Wherefore justice has great force among gods and men alike, since this virtue holds together the commonwealth of the All and the Whole, as found among both gods and men.[6]

We have come back, not only to the conception that a man's reason must dominate his lower powers, but to the thought that this subjective regimentation is to be called either virtue or justice and that such justice means that a man has properly harmonized himself with the organization of the universe. So Theages goes on to call the universal principle with which we attune ourselves the *orthos logos,* "the right reason," a term familiar in the Hellenistic world for the law of nature:

And in general what is not in tune with the *orthos logos* is vice. . . . But the alignment of the soul with the *orthos logos,* which manifests itself in the act of examining and passing judgment, is called intelligence; when it manifests itself in the enduring [of pains and the resisting of] pleasures, it is called self-control; when in eschewing gain and injury of one's neighbor, justice. Alignment of the soul with the *orthos logos,* as well as departure from it, is a matter of endeavor for what is necessary and of shunning what is not necessary. The necessary is what needs to be;

[6] The translation is taken from my *By Light, Light* (New Haven: 1935), p. 404; the fragment is found in Stobaeus, *op. cit.,* III.76 ff. (III.i. 117 f.).

42

and this allows no adding or taking away, for it is itself what needs must be. There are two forms of the unnecessary, namely, excess and lack. And excess is more than is necessary; lack is less than is necessary. But virtue is a state of the necessary, wherefore it is immediately a state of the extreme and the mean. It is a state of the extreme in that it contains what is necessary and of the mean by the fact that it lies between excess and lack. . . . But, since ethical virtue concerns the passions, and pleasure and pain are the highest forms of sensation, virtue would lie, not in the eradication of sensation, pleasure, and pain from the soul, but in the tuning of these together. For health, which is a proper mixture of the faculties of the body, consists, not in the eradication of the hot, cold, wet, and dry, but in their blending since it is a sort of symmetry of these. Similarly in music, concord exists, not by the eradication of the high and low tones, but by their somehow being tuned to each other. For, when the high and low are attuned, concord is achieved and discord banished; and, when the hot, cold, wet, and dry are tuned together, health arises and illness perishes. So when the spirited part and the desire have been tuned together, vices and passions disappear, while virtues and good dispositions arise. The distinguishing characteristic of the virtue of the good disposition is choice exercised in noble matters. It is possible to use reason and power even without virtue, but it is impossible to use choice, for choice indicates the worth of the disposition. Wherefore the reason, by forceful domination of the spirited and desiring parts, introduces continence and endurance, but when, on the contrary, reason itself is forcefully dominated by the unreasoning part, incontinence and weakness arise. Such states of the soul are only half perfect as either virtues or vices, for the reason is in the one case healthy, but the unreasoning parts of the soul are ill. And, insofar as the spirited and desiring parts are ruled and led by the part of the soul that has reason, continence and endurance can be regarded as virtues; but, insofar as this happens to them forcibly rather than by their own volition, continence and virtue are evils. For virtue ought to do the necessary things not painfully, but with pleasure. And, again, insofar as the spirited and desiring parts dominate the reason and so introduce weakness and incontinence, they are to be regarded as evils; but, insofar as, along with the [endurance of] pains, they gratify the passions yet recognizing that they are in error because the eye of the soul is still functioning properly, in this they are not evils. So, again, the same thing is clear, that virtue must do the necessary things voluntarily. The involuntary is never without pain and fear, but the voluntary is never without pleasure and good cheer. . . . For knowledge and vision of matters is the prerogative of the reasoning part of the soul. But power is the prerogative of the unreasoning part, for the power to endure pain and control pleasure is the property of the unreasoning part of the soul. But choice involves both of these—both the reasoning and unreasoning parts of the soul. For choice is made up out of the combination of intelligence and impulse, and of these intelligence belongs to the reasoning part, impulse to the unreasoning. Wherefore every virtue consists in a tuning together of the parts of the soul, and virtue involves altogether the voluntary and the power of choice.[7]

Reason may "forcibly dominate" the lower parts to make them take the road of endurance and continence set for them by nature as what is "necessary," but that is not the ideal way. The ideal way is such a handling of the lower instincts that they work in spontaneous harmony with the judgments of reason. After the analogy of the best medical theory of the day (which he directly quoted) as well as of our own day, Theages called this the health of the soul and believed that only in such cooperation of the parts of the

[7] *By Light, Light*, pp. 405 f.; Stobaeus, *loc. cit.* (III.i.118).

soul did one find liberty or the voluntary. This was probably an invasion of Stoic concepts, since the Stoics, too,
thought that, of all humanity, only the Wise Man was
free. The Pythagoreans as a whole had little interest in the
problem of freedom in even this limited sense; they were
still seeking how the mind could get such a grasp of the
higher reality that its vision would automatically put order
and harmony into the whole life of man.

"Intelligence is nothing but an understanding of happiness
in life," says Archytas[8] "or of the natural good of man." An
anonymous Pythagorean wrote:

> Law is to the soul and life of man what attunement is to
> hearing and sound. For law educates the soul and organizes
> life, while attunement makes the hearing intelligent and
> the sound unified.[9]

Still another Pythagorean, said in this case to be Aisara, the
daughter of Pythagoras himself, is quoted:

> Human nature seems to me to be the norm of law and
> justice, as well as of the household and the city. For if any
> one should track out and seek the traces in himself, he
> would find them. For there is law in himself, as well as
> justice—the orderly arrangement of the soul.[10]

Aisara goes on in this fragment to describe the typical threefold nature of the soul, which may be harmonized. She
closes the section by defining justice.

> I mean by perfect justice that state in which each part is
> aligned according to the attuning principle, proportion.
> And agreement and single-mindedness follow upon such
> an alignment. Such a condition would properly be called
> a well-lawed organization of the soul, which, from the fact

8 Stobaeus, *op. cit.*, III.63 (III.i.112).
9 *Ibid.*, IV.82 (IV.i.135).
10 *Ibid.*, I.355 (I.xlix.27).

that the better part is being the ruler and the worse part is being ruled, introduces into the soul the power of virtue.[11]

These passages show how almost monotonous was the repetition that man is a composite whose supreme virtue or goal is subjective harmony. The virtue in its logical sense was defined as justice, the regulation of the lower parts by the higher, reason.

Like most of the Greek philosophers, these Pythagoreans seem to have stopped their philosophizing by describing this ideal state. They offered no direct way of approaching it. Since they required that their pupils have a great deal of technical training, one may assume that, within the schools themselves, the method of training resembled Plato's, if, indeed, Plato had not himself derived his training from the Pythagoreans. It consisted in drill in the best science and mathematics of the day. Apparently, like many modern educational theorists, the Pythagoreans hoped that from such study the light of moral and metaphysical perception would illuminate the novitiate's soul. The solution worked very well, perhaps, for the scholars of the day, and to it we shall finally return, for it seems to me the best solution for the modern scholar as well. As still today, however, it had little appeal or use for the average man. If order was to be put into his soul it could not come from his contemplating the order of the universe, since such contemplation lay as far beyond his power of perception as of his imitation. There had to be an agency, a direct connection, revelation, savior, with whom or which he could identify himself in personal or ritualistic piety.

Accordingly, just as the Stoics projected the fulfillment of their desires into a fabulous Wise Man, the Pythagoreans looked to the divine king to be a revelation, a presentation,

[11] *Ibid.*, 357.

of cosmic law which would really put the souls of his subjects in order. This king, said one of the Pythagoreans, Ecphantus:

> is like the rest [of mankind] indeed in his earthly tabernacle, inasmuch as he is formed of the same material, but he is fashioned by the supreme Artificer, who, in making the king, used himself as the archetype.[12]

For more details of Pythagorean ideals of the king, I must refer the reader to an earlier study of mine.[13] Here, I need only assure him that there is a considerable body of quite surprising material to show that, for the Pythagoreans, if not for the Hellenistic world in general, the actual king, like Plato's philosopher-king to whom the ideal was closely related, was the means God provided to bring the supreme unwritten law of God's own nature into the human realm. In place of tabulated legislation, man could find the principle of divine right, incarnate and made personal and adaptable, in the person of the king, who was called therefore "the animate and vocal law." God rules the world, it is said, not by a set of laws, but by presenting to it his own person, which at once inspires the cosmos to imitate him. God's person is the law, not the laws, of nature. The trouble with men is that most of them have no perception of this divine model and so must be governed by law in the derivative form of laws. This is necessity, compulsion. To counterbalance this, God gives man the divine king, in whom the law, or Logos (in this sense of "Law," the two are quite synonymous), is miraculously incarnate.

> Oh, that it were possible to put from human nature all need for obedience! The fact that, as mortal animals, we

[12] *Ibid.*, IV.272 (IV.vii.64), as translated in my "The Political Philosophy of Hellenistic Kingship," *Yale Classical Studies*, I (1928), 76.
[13] *Loc. cit.*

47

are not exempt from it is the basest trace of our earthiness, inasmuch as a deed of obedience is very close to being one of necessity, for what just escapes being brought about by the one is produced by the other. Whatever things can by their own nature use the beautiful have no occasion for obedience, since they have no fear of necessity. The king alone is capable of putting this good into human nature, so that by imitation of him, their better, they will follow in the way they should go. But his Logos, if it is accepted, strengthens those who have been corrupted by evil nurture as if by drink and who have fallen into forgetfulness; it heals the sick, drives out this forgetfulness which has settled on them as a result of their sin, and makes memory live in its place, from which so-called obedience springs. Taking thus its beginning from seeds of trifling import, this grows to be something excellent, even in an earthly environment, in which the Logos, associating with man, restores what has been lost by sin.[14]

That is, man finds himself not free, but a slave to compulsions, what today we should call compulsive neuroses. Like us, the author of this fragment, Ecphantus, recognized that inner and outer compulsions arise from wrong experiences, "wrong education," in youth. The cure is not in enforced legal obedience to precepts, since this is only another sort of compulsion, but in spontaneously imitating the law of nature, the nature of God, or the Logos—whatever you wish to call it. In this way, we shall find freedom from compulsion of every sort—freedom which is ours only when our natures thus reflect Nature. But it is saving knowledge which we need, a saving vision of what that Nature is. The Hellenistic world increasingly came to feel that this could be found only by revelation, here revelation in a God-given person who should incarnate the Logos, in this case the king.

[14] Stobaeus, *op. cit.*, IV.278 (IV.vii.65), as translated in my "Hellenistic Kingship," p. 89.

"To look at the king should put one in order like the music of a flute," said one of the Pythagoreans.[15] True, the actual king rarely justified such a description of his person or of his effect on his subjects, but the dream persisted, appeared in Philo and in such a Neo-Platonist as Proclus: became the basis of the theory of monarchy in Roman law; and is still represented by the pontiff in Rome, whose prerogatives, if not officially his person, are a direct survival of this conception.

The modern world is still haunted by this same dream, despite the failures of Hitler and Mussolini. The Athenians sang to Demetrius Poliorcetes:

> The other gods are far away, have no ears, do not exist at all, or pay no attention to us. Thee we see face to face, not in wood or stone, but living and in truth. And so we pray to thee: "First give us peace." [16]

The United States has no ideal king or queen, as the British still have to embody their emotional loyalties; but no man could be elected president of the United States whom election propaganda had not built up, at least for the majority of voters, as a personal embodiment of American ideals.

Here we are concerned with this ideal only to see how the people of the age, even the stern Hellenistic philosophers, were looking for divine persons. Men had at first wanted to find their saving knowledge in direct metaphysical perception, then in the laws of states; but these had both failed. The laws of physics and mathematics should suggest the laws of the universe, which are themselves moral laws, they all believed; but many people at the end of the brilliant scientific advance of the Hellenistic age were haunted by such a sense of failure as many feel today. New perceptions

[15] Stobaeus, *op. cit.*, IV.265 f. (IV.vii.62); "Hellenistic Kingship," p. 72.
[16] Athenaeus *Deipnosophists* VI.63 (253ᵈ⁻ᵗ).

of physical, mathematical, and moral reality did not bring new moral insights to the people. Accordingly, many turned to the ideal Person, who should save men by being the incarnate Logos. For this reason, when Caesar and then Augustus offered men what was really a fascist state, with one man taking full responsibility for the moral judgments of the world, the world was ready to hail him as the divine ruler who had come at last to end their search.

The victory of this idea, that moral, psychological, and religious questions are settled in the person of an imperator or *Führer*, meant, of course, the beginning of the end of classical civilization. We cannot be saved by the virtues of our human rulers, however much they may suggest divinity. Unless we isolate them from actual political power, as do the English, their divinity becomes, not a helpful painted curtain, but a mirage to lead us to destruction. Plato and Aristotle rightly saw that, even if some one individual could, by his extraordinary knowledge and character, safely be allowed to take over the powers and decisions of society, nature would provide him with no successors. British monarchy is so successful because, although the king or queen is the focus of projected, and so of creative, idealism, the actual ruler has little power. The monarch can indeed be helpful as an embodied myth, but he becomes a menace if he has power also.

A popular version of the quest for saving knowledge had also appeared in the Hellenistic mystery religions. Here, groups of people offered to give the real truth to men for a round fee, a truth dispensed in initiations in which the candidate identified himself with the god, put on his robes, died and rose with him in pantomime, and learned the secret passwords which would take him past the cosmic censors to heavenly bliss. So far as I know, this type of solution had little original or inherent association with the more philosophic approach we are briefly tracing, though its conceptions influenced philosophers from Plato, if not from Heraclitus and Pythagoras, down. Plutarch, and probably many like him, by allegory of myths and rites identified the saving knowledge of these psychological theories with the myths of Dionysus and Isis.

In Philo we suddenly find all this presented together, and with a new and joyous announcement that saving knowledge was to be found in "divine men" of whom the Greek world had never heard.

Philo may be briefly identified as a Jew who lived in Alexandria, exactly contemporary with Jesus. He was born some fifteen years before Jesus and died perhaps a little more than that after Jesus' death. His extensive writings are designed to show how Judaism, especially in the writings of Moses, anticipated Greek philosophy and mystery religion by offering all that seemed best to Philo in Greek civilization, ethics, law, and mysticism. Philo read all this into the books of Moses by interpreting them in fantastic allegories, for, like all apologists, he had less interest in what the writings said than in what he could project into them. With him, and in all probability with a whole school of which he was only the chief spokesman, all of this religious psychology went into the Judaism of at least some Jews.

Philo, too, found the human personality to be a mixture of "bodily" desires and divine nature. The plurality of the psyche, for which he had no fixed scheme, made for him, as for his predecessors, a "city" in which the lower members act as centers of compulsion. The one hope is that reason rule the lower members. These members have laws of their own, laws that each fulfill and gratify their own functions, just as a "good" stomach will bring us to the table with a good appetite. Such recognition of the value of desire recalls Plato and the Pythagoreans, rather than the Stoics. The members also have collectively a real mind of their own to justify their demands, and this lower, or bodily, mind recalls Aristotle. In contrast, the higher, or true, mind, in the opinion of Philo as of the Greeks, is a divine fragment, or presence, in the individual. Lost in the middle, somewhere between the essentially physical and the essentially divine, or immaterial, parts, is the integrating factor, which with him becomes clearly recognizable for the first time as the ego.

> We have ourselves, and all that goes to make these selves, as a loan, *I* [the ego], indeed, am a combination of soul [here mind, or divine part] and body. I seem to have mind, reason [or speech], and sense perception, yet I find that none of these is my own property. For where was my body before *I* was born, and whither will it go when *I* have died? . . . Whence came the soul, and whither will it go, and how long will it live with *us?* Can we tell what is its essential nature? And when did *we* come to possess it? Before birth? But then *we* did not exist. After death? But then *we*, who in our junction with our bodies are mixtures and have qualities, shall not exist but shall be brought into the rebirth, by which, becoming joined to immaterial things, we shall become unmixed and without qualities.[17]

The ego within all this is clearly for Philo, the weakest member. It is really a worm between chickens, each of which tries to dominate the other and take the ego captive. When the ego identifies itself with either the body or the reason, the other becomes powerless. The higher mind within us, Philo tells us elsewhere, has immediate access to metaphysical truth, the law of God or nature in its pure form. But man's higher mind can function only as the ego unites with it to dominate the lower mind or functions. The

[17] *De Cherubim*, 113 ff. See my *By Light, Light*, p. 375.

higher mind is, indeed, the presence of God himself in a man, and it is strengthened as it goes out from itself into God. It must constantly war against the "empty opinion" of the lower mind. The lower mind, he said, like the builders of the Tower of Babel, dares to hope that it can rise by what we should call empirical methods to a comprehension and mastery of the heavenly regime, which is indeed blasphemy. The lower mind is the "bestial mind" in man which fortifies the citadel of man against his own self. It is the king of Egypt, which enslaves the true Israelites—who are collectively the higher mind—and makes them wait on the Egyptians—the passions. Or the lower mind is the inhabitants of Sodom resisting the attempt of Lot—here the higher mind—to reform their Sodomitic practices. The Sodomites, in Philo's telling, protested in words which have a strangely familiar sound. As the bodily desires, the libido, they do not want Lot to rule over them: "For our territory is licentiousness, and sensual pleasure is our law and legitimate will." [18] On the other hand, if the divine nature flows into a man who has this sort of anarchy, the lower nature is put to rout.

> When there comes into the soul, as into a land, the prudence of a keen-eyed and seeing nature, all the gentile laws which are in it become mad and rage and turn aside from worthy thoughts, for evil things are unable to dwell and live together with good ones.[19]

But licentiousness itself, he says, is something quite in accordance with the law of nature, for by it our bodies are preserved.[20] That is, it is a law of the nature of the flesh to seek its own gratification. The law is quite inevitable, be-

[18] *Quaestiones in Genesin* iv.39; cf. *By Light, Light,* p. 392. This work of Philo is preserved only in an Armenian translation; I quote from the translation of Ralph Marcus in the Loeb Classical Library (Cambridge; Harvard University Press).
[19] *Quaestiones in Exodum* ii.22; cf. *By Light, Light,* p. 392.
[20] *Quaest. Gen.* ii.46.

cause only by hunger and thirst can the body express and satisfy its basic needs. The other bodily impulses similarly have their proper function according to the natural laws of the body. But, since all material nature should be subject to the immaterial law of nature, the impulses of any of our members must often be restrained.

In a sense, there is a conflict within nature itself between the law of the nature of the part and the law of nature for the whole, so that Philo returns to the Pythagorean solution, in which the cosmos itself consists of a tuning together, a harmony, of conflicting forces. In man, these two aspects of natural law clash—the law of the whole and the laws proper for each member. Nature can produce harmony only as it subordinates the particular drives, and similarly in man the higher law, represented by his reason as the Logos within him, must dominate and attune the laws of the senses and body and thereby produce the inner harmony which is "justice." So Philo says that we must abandon war, that is, necessity, what comes into existence and passes away, so that we can go over to the unbegotten or changeless and the voluntary.[21] Philo passionately aspired to win this justice in the soul. The process of achieving it involves increasingly identifying one's higher mind with the divine mind. We live, not "to ourselves," but "to God" or "according to nature," in which case the highest nature—human, cosmic, and divine—are all one.

Although ideally one achieves this by identifying one's own mind with the divine mind, in fact man cannot do so without help from God. Philo gloats over the pagans, because, as a Jew, he has help of which they know nothing. First, and on a lower level, he has the perfect legislation codified under God himself which Pindar and later Plato and Aristotle looked to for the healing of the nations. But

[21] *De Somniis* ii.253.

Philo's *Pentateuch* offered not merely the dubious salvation of legal precepts, observant a Jew as Philo himself always was. Far more important to him, his Bible told him of actual incarnations of the Logos, men who were truly the animate law, in a sense that the Pythagorean "king" and the Stoic "wise man" could represent only in fancy. For in the great patriarchs, especially Moses, God had actually taken the initiative and brought to mankind those saving paragons. Philo taught that, when an individual was "initiated by Moses," he could be identified with them or, rather, with the Spirit, or Logos, they incarnated. Thereby he would get the divine life and power Moses brought to man, the life and power which would make justice, the subjective victory, possible in his own soul. It was not a matter of "trying" or "willing." The saving act was God's, not ours. Ours was the saving attitude of acceptance and surrender, which would lead to an orientation in God that Philo called *pistis*, "faith."

Philo designed much of his writing to show how the patriarchs were either born in this perfect condition, as Isaac and Moses had been, or came to it by migration as Abraham from Ur, Jacob from his home, the Israelites from Egypt, that is, out from the domination of the body to such a full translation into the realm of God that the migrants themselves became Wise Men or the incarnation of the Logos as ideal kings. By identifying ourselves with them, which we could do much more easily than we could identify with the metaphysical God or law, we could win the same victory, make the same migration.

Before going on to Paul, whose psychology and conception of salvation is intelligible only from the point of view of the material we have been discussing, I should like to stop just a moment to show from a striking myth why I think that, consciously or unconsciously, the ancient world was generally and popularly thinking in the same way—that man is saved as the ego directly accepts the ideal, the god, and by this new power conquers the lower desires. The myth is vividly told in a dithyrambic hymn, the Seventh Homeric Hymn,[22] which is addressed to Dionysus and so which probably reflects popular Orphism. I cannot hope that the details of the hymn are familiar, and they are so striking that I must quote it entire.

> I will tell of Dionysus, the son of glorious Semele, how he appeared on a jutting headland by the shore of the fruitless sea, seeming like a stripling in the first flush of manhood: his rich, dark hair was waving about him, and on his strong shoulders he wore a purple robe. Presently there came swiftly over the sparkling sea Tyrsenian pirates on a well-decked ship; a miserable doom led them on. When they saw him they made signs to one another and sprang out quickly and, seizing him straightway, put him on board their ship exultingly; for they thought him the son of heaven-nurtured kings. They sought to bind him with rude bonds, but the bonds would not hold him, and the withes fell far away from his hands and feet; and he sat with a smile in his dark eyes. Then the helmsman understood all and cried out at once to his fellows and said:
>
> "Madmen! What god is this whom you have taken and bind, strong that he is? Not even the well-built ship can carry him. Surely this is either Zeus or Apollo, who has the silver bow, or Poseidon, for he looks not like mortal men but like the gods who dwell on Olympus. Come, then, let us set him free upon the dark shore at once; do not lay hands on him, lest he grow angry and stir up dangerous winds and heavy squalls."

[22] This is the translation, with a few minor changes, in Hugh G. Evelyn-White, *Hesiod, The Homeric Hymns and Homerica* (New York: Loeb Classical Library, 1914), pp. 428–433.

So said he; but the skipper chid him with taunting words: "Madman, mark the wind and help hoist sail on the ship; catch all the sheets. As for this fellow, we men will see to him; I reckon he is bound for Egypt or for Cyprus or to the Hyperboreans or farther still. But in the end he will speak out and tell us his friends and all his wealth and his brothers, now that providence has thrown him in our way."

When he had said this, he had mast and sail hoisted on the ship, and the wind filled the sail, and the crew hauled taut the sheets on either side. But soon strange things were seen among them. First of all, a sweet fragrant wine ran streaming throughout all the black ship and a heavenly smell arose, so that all the seamen were seized with amazement when they saw it. And all at once a vine spread out both ways along the top of the sail with many clusters hanging down from it, and a dark ivy plant twined about the mast, blossoming with flowers and with rich berries growing on it; and all the thole-pins were covered with garlands. When the pirates saw all this, then at last the skipper bade the helmsman to put the ship to land. But the god changed into a dreadful lion there on the ship, in the bows, and roared loudly; amidships, also, he showed his wonders and created a shaggy bear which stood up ravening, while on the forepeak was the lion glaring fiercely with scowling brows. And so the sailors fled into the stern and crowded bemused about the right-minded helmsman, until suddenly the lion sprang upon the skipper and seized him; and when the sailors saw it they leapt out overboard one and all into the bright sea, escaping from a miserable fate, and were changed into dolphins. But on the helmsman Dionysus had mercy and held him back and made him altogether happy, saying to him:

"Be of good cheer, my good man; you have found favor with my heart. I am loud-crying Dionysus whom Cadmus' daughter, Semele, bare of union with Zeus."

Hail child of fair-faced Semele! He who forgets thee can in no wise compose sweet song.

Here is the threefold division we have been meeting in so many places. The pirate ship is the personality manned primarily by bodily desires. It is headed by the skipper, who may be called the "bodily mind." A helmsman steers the ship, but the skipper completely dominates him and forces him to work with the other sailors. He is essentially different, however, for when the god, the higher divine element, comes into the boat, the helmsman alone recognizes him. The skipper and the other pirates want to bind the divinity and use him for their own ends, but that, since this is a myth of the saving power of the god, is impossible. The god asserts himself, kills the skipper, changes the desires into dolphins, and fills the ship with himself. Only the helmsman is preserved. Now, in the new adjustment, the helmsman, that is, the reason, and the god together constitute the personality, and only harmless dolphins, themselves love symbols, remain to recall the old compulsions of the desires. The ego is now as much the servant of the god as formerly of the piratical desires. "For me to live is Dionysus" might well have been the final word; instead, in more psychological language, the poem finally declares that harmony can come only from a soul which has been thus itself harmonized. The culmination of the experience was expressed in one of the most beautiful of Greek vase paintings.

We have found the basic Greek concept variously expressed. It assumed the essential multiplicity of the parts of the soul and the necessity that they be brought into harmony. This psychology or scheme of salvation Paul took for granted and carefully expounded, especially in the seventh and eighth chapters of Romans. He, too, describes a vague lot of "members," each with a law driving it to its gratification and fulfillment. Collectively, the members or desires are represented by a "mind of the flesh," called in another passage "our old man." The "mind of the flesh" is extremely active and clever and, under ordinary circumstances, is quite able to defeat the "mind of the spirit," "the inward man," "my mind," which recognizes and introduces into man a higher law only to see it flouted by the "flesh." Between these two "I" stand, a weak little member like the helmsman; "I" recognize the higher life but must take orders from the fleshly skipper. "The good which I would I do not: but the evil which I would not, that I practice." [23]

Paul, like Philo, considered that God himself had acted to help man overcome this tragic helplessness of the ego by sending the cosmic law, or Logos, to the earth in human form, incarnate. For Paul, that incarnation was not Moses and the patriarchs, but the "law of the spirit which is in Christ Jesus." Paul, like Philo, however, appropriated the divine figure by identification. Paul did not use the term, but he was initiated into Jesus as he identified himself with Jesus' death and resurrection, and as a consequence Paul's inner realm was entirely reconstituted. The "mind of the flesh" died within him; he had put to death the "deeds of the body," since now his "mind of the spirit," or higher part, had taken into itself the "law of the spirit of life in Christ Jesus" and so at last had power to dominate, as Dionysus had had in the boat. But, just as the pirates were given a new life as dolphins, so the savior in Paul "redeemed the body," gave a new type of life also to his mortal body. Now, indeed, for Paul "to live is Christ." Paul was fully Greek in calling this new experience "justice," the state of inner adjustment and harmony. So he no longer felt any "condemnation" or, as

[23] Rom. 7:19.

we would say "guilt," for Paul was freed from the compulsive neurosis which he vividly called "the law of sin and death."

We shall return to Paul's experience in a later chapter, but, in all of this development, we have been watching the Greeks increasingly orient their religion to the best psychology of the day. Men seemed to abandon the hope that rational discipline or education would lead them to such a perception of ultimate truth that it would harmonize the conflicts of the soul. Instead, a new hope arose—that God would take the initiative and offer metaphysical reality in a human incarnation, whether in the Wise Man, king, Moses, or Christ, and that, by identifying ourselves with this person or by accepting the benefit of his revelation and nature, we may all come into saving knowledge and "justice."

Salvation was for the early Christians still a matter of bringing the "higher mind" to such "saving knowledge" that it would take the ego into itself, rule the desires and lower mind completely, and so give man inner harmony. The difference between religion and the rationalist psychiatry of the ancients has proved to be a difference of means rather than of ends. Indeed, as one reads the passionate descriptions of the rational process in Plato's *Phaedrus* and in the cave of the *Republic,* one wonders whether the rationalistic approach is not simply one of the techniques of religion, rather than something which one must always distinguish from religion. For Plato, too, we must never forget, could climb by love.

After Paul, however, Christians lost interest in, and soon even comprehension of, this psychological tradition. They developed a new psychology which completely abandoned the older centers of compulsion and instead regarded man as psychologically made up of "faculties," intellect, feeling, and will. The old psychology completely disappeared. James Ropes of Harvard told me years ago that clearly, even from the time of John Chrysostom, no Christians understood what Paul was talking about when he spoke of "the law of the members." To a considerable extent, it was Paul himself who quite unwittingly founded the new psychology or at least suggested it.

Quite apart from what we have been discussing, it appears that Paul had to defend his new faith from a number of attacks. One of these seems to have been that it was nonsense to suppose that the "justice" of a single savior or individual could correct the sinful pathology of the race and of cosmos itself. Paganism offered many saviors, as did hellenized Jews in their many patriarchs. It seemed foolish to think that the "righteousness of one man" would answer for the race.

Paul met this as Philo would have done, by finding a passage in Scripture which he could allegorize into an explanation. So he devised the clever allegory[24] that, since all men are sinners as a result of the disobedience of a single person, Adam, from whom we all descend, so it is clear that, by the perfect obedience of one man, the curse from Adam could be removed as men became new creatures in Christ. The allegory was in all probability a pure *tour de force* whose consistency with his general thinking had little importance. Philo has scores of such allegories of the moment. But, to the Christian Fathers, all that Paul wrote was literally and ponderously true, and so out of this allegory of the fall grew the momentous doctrine of original sin, the fallen "will." Sin became primarily not maladjustment but disobedience, and salvation, a problem of restoring to the will the power to obey, to obey, not God as represented in the "law of one's mind," but God as revealed and made available in revelation.

[24] He discusses this primarily in Rom. 5:12–21, but seems to allude to it in passing in I Cor. 15:45.

Christianity repeatedly returns to this, as it has been doing since Karl Barth, with the feeling that we have the truth and need only a new "heart" to obey it.

Modern psychology has brought us back to much of the ancient point of view, and this we shall consider in Chapter Three. Here, however, we have a sample of the way in which thoughtful people in the past have used, as we must use, the best knowledge available to make formulations they could live by. Paul transferred to Christ the psychological ideas that thoughtful hellenized Jews used in explaining religious experience. Paul's and John's evaluation of the person of Jesus, that he brought to men the Logos, or law of the Spirit, in human form, was as much a mythological design on a curtain as were Plato's figures of the chariot or cave or as the hope of a divine king by the Pythagoreans and Dio Chrysostom or as Philo's descriptions of Abraham and Moses. We can still feel a kinship with them, however, as we see how they tried to explain man's religious experience by the best their generations knew.

We have, indeed, returned to the conception that, if man is seeking happiness and integrity of character, he must find them in the structure of his own psyche. We are now struggling with various suggestions as to how man can create in himself the ability to "sing sweet song," sing to himself and to others. The terror of the tremendum without and of the anarchy of conflicting standards and desires within is still our terror. We, too, crave to come into the peace and dignity that "justice" meant to Plato and Paul, and we similarly know that in ignorance we blunder and that in knowledge of reality alone can we hope. Modern psychology, psychiatry, and sociology no longer assume that we have that knowledge through biblical and ecclesiastical revelation. On the other hand, we are today not so rationalist as Plato often sounds (or is made to sound) and as the savants of the eighteenth century actually were. Still, we are convinced that only better knowledge can give man hope—better knowledge, indeed, of precisely those matters which all these ancients were so passionately exploring.

3

Psychological
Assumptions

MODERN PSYCHOLOGY HAS TAUGHT us that a man's personality is by no means to be identified with his consciousness,
that is, with those attitudes, subjective states, ideas, or motives of which he is aware. The permanent contributions of
Freud have been summarized as being, first, that psychic
processes are strictly determined; second, that actions and
feelings, as well as thoughts or ideas, may be determined by
unconscious motivations, motivations which often astonish
the individual when and if his "conscious mind" at last discovers them; and, third, that our motivations are emotional

forces. These are permanent contributions because so far as I know, all modern schools of psychology or psychiatry accept them, in however different terms each may describe the mechanism involved.

The chief doubt would be as to whether the first of the three—the statement that all our mental processes are strictly determined, with the assumption that man has no freedom of will—does not go a bit beyond the evidence. Empirical investigation has to assume a complete process of cause and effect within the psyche (as in all other scientific investigation), but that is a working hypothesis which, though it works very well, does not justify us in finally begging the question to the point that we assert that all our vivid sense of a power of choice is illusion. It is, however, now beyond dispute that the greater part, at least, of our psychic processes are determined by our physical nature and our early experiences as we react to external stimuli. Jung added to this that "the unconscious," far from being simply a repository of rejected and repressed experiences which are harmful to the personality, include also many drives and guiding motives which are among our best influences to good.

A second chief contribution of modern psychology seems to me its unwitting revival of the ancient notion we have been discussing, the notion that the personality consists of quite independent centers of emotional compulsion, almost independent minor personalities, each with rational power or power of rationalization and each in such conflict with the others that they tend to develop tensions and conflicts within us. Psychic ill health may then be defined in terms of the Jungian one-sidedness, the Freudian obsessional complexes, or the "conditioning" to conflicting reflexes. The three seem basically names for the same thing, since all mean that health is a full life of the whole man and that inner balance, harmony, or mutual adjustment of the parts to one another can alone produce such an inner adjustment that one can face environmental problems realistically and objectively.

The modern schools disagree quite as sharply as did the ancient ones as to what these divisions are and should be called. The schools are not consistent within themselves, so far as I can see; for example, I do not see any relation between Freud's ego-id-superego and his conscious, preconscious, and subconscious minds. To an outsider, however, modern thought seems pretty well agreed in assuming two basic focuses of ideational-emotional concentration and compulsion. Without prejudice to the other schools, we may with the Freudians call the first of these focuses the id, that part of man which is most akin to what Paul called the old man, the flesh, or the members, which he thought have their own laws and mind. The id constitutes the personality of the new-born baby, which simply wants its physical desires gratified; the id fully takes over again with some of the greatest of human beings if they fall into senile decay. The id is with all of us always and is the psychological concomitant of what theology calls "the old Adam," or original sin. In its pure infantile form, it is completely indifferent to the inconvenience of its parents and only wants what it wants when it wants it. This personality within us seems never to be socialized. It may be repressed, guided, thwarted, but continues in every person as a quite irresponsible craving for direct gratification of purely selfish urges. In itself, it contemplates murder, rape, robbery, or any chicanery with complete indifference. But it is the *élan vital* within one. A man without a powerful id is a psychological eunuch, colorless and spiritually flabby.

If the baby had only this self-centered gratification as the basis of his personality, he would not last long. In his helplessness, he quickly learns that he is part of, depends utterly upon, a larger entity. He begins to feel that his mother or the mother-father restrict as well as gratify him. They become, like God or the Pythagorean kings, personalities whose very personalities are laws for him, and he finds that even the gratification of the desires of his id depends largely on his adjusting to the demands of those larger natures. The experience is not merely frustrating, for the id discovers that one of the sweetest of its own gratifications is the pleasure of the mother's smiling approval and caresses. Without understanding a bit of this, the infant is like a young cat or chicken in that he needs the mother or the protection of a mother-substitute for his very existence. His psychological nature forces him to comply to her, for the sense of the mother's protection gives him happiness, and, when he feels estranged, alone, he is terrified. Like the young animal, he lapses into panic when this umbilical cord of his emotions, the sense of protection from the mother or mother-father, is threatened.

Now, in raising chickens we may substitute artificial heat for mother warmth and so raise chickens that do not need the mother; but that is not nature's way, and we have not yet such artificial brooders for human infants. A young fox can be brought up by its mother or, if taken early enough, by man. But the fox nursed by men with a bottle will have a very different personality from the fox that grows up with its mother; the one will be tame, the other wild. Normally, the little fox takes on the fears, prejudices, and patterns of the mother fox. Similarly, what makes a child into an Arapahoe Indian, or a little Chinese, or American, is the planting in him by the mother-father, then by society at large, of a whole pattern of behavior. The Freudians use one terminology for this new pattern and its ramifications, the neurologists another, the stimulus–response people still another. But all essentially agree that this socializing process (the capacity for which may lie in a special part of the brain) produces what acts as a counterpersonality in the psyche as over against the id. The new personality is primarily the ingestion of the personality of the mother-father until it becomes a part of the child's own inner nature, however much it may be complicated by stimuli from other social experiences as time goes on. It functions within him as a new center of compulsion. The main function of this new center is to continue the work of the mother-father in controlling the antisocial desires of the id. This center we may call a man's "social center," in contrast to his id, the personal one, though the name is not altogether satisfactory.

The social center leads us to conform to the society that we immediately experience. Its business is to give us the security of conformity, of "belonging" and being accepted. For this, one will indeed curb the desires of one's id. In a savage society which narrowly fixes standards of conduct and where perhaps no one has questioned them for thousands of years, each individual gets much the same standards of social living from his parents as from his young companions, so that the social center which he builds up in himself or which experiences and inferences build up in him is quite like that of most other members of the tribe. The more complex the society and the experiences of the individual in it, however, the less uniform are the standards and the resulting compulsions of the social center. The child in any but the lowest criminal environment of our civilization or, less commonly, in what considers itself our top social stratum learns and incorporates as part of himself one pattern of values from his parents, or perhaps several patterns, since they, like him, have not been made into a unit in their social centers. He learns another from his schoolmates on the sand lot or behind the bushes; another, from his growing acquaintance with the critical study of man and his own society as he studies and reads; still another, from his priest or rabbi; and others, in turn as he goes out into business or joins a country club. These patterns may in fact amount to a number of social centers within him, rather nastily at war among themselves because he responds differently to different patterns in different environments. As between the demands of his business standards and those of his church, he may get into painful suspense.

Occasionally, a strong character rejects this pluralism by developing a single positive social center, in the name of which or from whose strength he can defy practically all the conventions of society. Such a man becomes an "odd Dick," one who "goes his own way." Like the prophets, Jesus, and Socrates, he may go completely contrary to the dominant social trends of his group, do so in the name not of his id but of conformity to a divine obligation to flout human society though it kill him. Or, quite the reverse, his id may reject the social center completely, so that he steps out from an ideally socialized family to become a criminal. But, normally, the social center remains as early determined, though it be a plurality of centers. Such plurality appears, of course, so much more commonly than a single and united one that we may call the plurality the normal effect of complicated civilization on an individual.

The subjective socialization which has taken the place of the objective parents carries over from them the power to punish disobedience primarily by its power to invoke the old terror of insecurity in the child cut off from it. To this terror or chronic uneasiness which comes from the inner disapproval, we give the name "guilt." Consequently, just as one of the strongest drives of a young animal is to keep close to the approving mother, so one of the strongest compulsions within us in later years is to avoid a sense of guilt by getting and keeping a sense that we are righteous according to the standards of our social environment. It is no accident that Jews and Christians so much like the figure of finding salvation "under the shadow of thy wings." Guilt may result from a compulsory following of the id against the dictates of the social center, as it did in the case of Paul. But it may also come from a conflict among the various social centers within us, each of which presents a different standard of action for a given situation, so that to choose one means to take a beating from the others. A splendid example of this hell appeared in the state of mind of many of our conscientious objectors who, after deciding for or against going into the army, were eager for the most punitive assignments to assuage the sense of guilt which tortured them for having violated one of their social centers for another.

If a psychologically ill man is to recover, he must often abandon his old scale of values for a new one. It usually comes out that most of us have several such scales. In our environment, with its millenniums of conditioning in the language of monotheism, we do not personify these scales and call each a god. We reserve that term for the special social compulsion and its personification which we recognize consciously in church. That is a mere *façon de parler*. The ancients had a god for each, gods who were naturally jealous of one another. Hermes, the god of gain (and, of course, of theft) was not on the best of terms with Apollo or Zeus or Ares. The later philosophers of antiquity tried to unite these by asserting that they were all merely aspects of a single deity, as the Sabellians tried later to put intelligible unity into the Christian Trinity. The spirit of paganism continues active, since, if we can no longer personalize the socializing centers in stories of the gods, such personalities reappear with complete freedom in our dreams. A large proportion of neuroses are matters of divergent conceptions of how we are to get social security, with the patient like a distracted rat getting the shock of guilt as he turns to any possible solution of his problems.

We simply must run from these pains. We inevitably shun a path which promises to hurt us, since we live on the pleasure–pain principle, however strangely some of us take our pleasures. We should, if we are sufficiently balanced, be able to endure immediate pain in order to get greater reward at the end, but so much of our lives are motivated uncon-sciously that we find that some immediate desire, like the dipsomaniac's desire for quick release from some uncon-scious torture within him, sweeps aside all our best hedonic calculus. Accordingly, one may escape the agony of guilt by so completely identifying oneself with the personal de-sires, that the social impulse finally loses its power. Such a person "has no conscience," is quite "amoral," or is thor-oughly "autistic" or "narcissistic"—whatever you wish to call it. On the other hand, one may be so entirely under the compulsions of the social drive that the impulses of the id seem to have quite vanished, or at least those impulses have vanished which the social drive has been conditioned to condemn.

If the social drive, oriented in human society or God, suffi-ciently condemns sex, in general or in particular, the man or woman is incapable of the sexual act under particular cir-cumstances or at all. Such a condemnation appears in prac-tically all of us in the incest taboo, which operates so effec-tively that, despite our dreams' showing us our real attitudes, in conscious life we not only do not commit incest, but even the idea is unthinkable. Society, however, has by no means implanted such a finality, such an inevitability of guilt for infraction, in the case of most other sorts of sexual indul-gence which it condemns, and hence the superego has less

71

power in these circumstances, and temptation becomes stronger or irresistible as the desire is met by a weaker threat of guilt-punishment. But a perfectly normal man or woman, physically, may be utterly frigid if trained that way by parents or by a traumatic experience in childhood.

The modern conception of the psyche and its structure sounds, as I have described it, like the latest school in the procession of ancient psychologies we reviewed. Enriched incomparably beyond any of them, it still begins with the idea that the psyche consists of several centers of impulse. Like the ancient thinkers, the moderns speak as though each of these centers can produce reasons, has a mind of its own. We no longer say that the basic tension is between a divine and immaterial fragment as against a material body. But still the body and its needs, as represented in the id, face in the social center a rival which claims to speak to us in the name not only of society but of God, tells us that this or that is or is not in accordance with the divine nature or will, indeed tells us that it is God's own voice within us, and punishes us cruelly for disobedience.

For the modern as for the ancient, the healthy soul is one whose parts are adjusted to one another so that these conflicts and pains are minimized and, more positively, so that the personality as a whole, having made a social adjustment corresponding to its subjective one, can move freely in creative activity. Disregarding some recent attempts to solve the tensions of these parts of the soul by brain surgery, the modern psychiatric technique for attaining psychic health is, again like that of the ancients, not exhortation to follow precepts, but education. There are other techniques, of course—such as rest, temporary retirement, change of environment or occupation, shock—but in these the physician is essentially only clearing the road for nature itself to release the tensions. The active psychiatry, one may say, and certainly the one most distinctive of the recent development which produced the new psychology itself is education. But it must be self-education, one that leads the patient to discover in himself the existence of these various centers and the actual nature of the conflicting desires and fears. The hope is that, when a person actually learns what is going on within him, he will be able to free himself from destructive compulsions, reconcile warring impulses, and put all in order. Abraham Maslow recently wrote that one of the greatest discoveries of Freud, one often overlooked, was that, the more a man knows about his own nature, what he really desires and needs for satisfaction, the "more effortless, automatic, and epiphenomenal become his value choices." [1] The id will, ideally, no longer be frustrated or the social center flay one with the vengeful torture of guilt or anxiety as one comes to understand nature, social and physical, and especially one's own nature and its desires and possibilities within the larger nature.

Into this I need not go; I have not the slightest competence to expound therapy for psychological difficulties. What I do want to point out is how this new-old theory of the structure of the soul illuminates the religious experiences of men. The hope is that, in doing so, one may come to understand better the religious experiences themselves and may even get some light on psychiatric problems, since, as I have said, religion has been the psychiatry of the ages and must always, so far as I can see, be the psychiatry of the masses.

Before we approach an analysis of the types of religious experience, however, a little more definition is necessary.

First, we must recall the great cleft in religious motivation which Paul Tillich once suggested to me when he ruled out as magic all religion whose motive was personal benefit. Fol-

---

[1] From a mimeographed copy of his "Fusion of Facts and Values," the Eleventh Annual Karen Horney Lecture (March 28, 1963), p. 6.

lowing what I said about magic in a previous chapter, I must
say that this was a metaphysical value judgment for which
a historian or empirical thinker has no use at all. Tillich
meant that religion as he himself conceives it should not include the attempt to get personal benefit. Like all of us,
Tillich has difficulty in distinguishing between his tastes and
what is now oddly often called "existential" reality. In point
of fact, most people have seen in religion a way of getting
something highly desirable which they might not otherwise
secure. We recall that Jesus himself taught us to pray for
our daily bread. Jews still celebrate Rosh Hashana and Yom
Kippur to get forgiveness, reconciliation, and a prosperous
new year; and Christians go to Mass for very concrete indulgences in a very concrete Purgatory. It has been good
business to be a deacon or vestryman in a prominent church.
In a famous Episcopal school, I have been reliably told, most
of the boys take Communion the Sunday before examinations. Protestants and Catholics alike have found that their
hold on the public is strongest when the public believes in a
vividly fiery hell that can be avoided only through rites or
practices offered by the church. I would not suggest for a
moment that Christianity is totally directed to such objective rewards; even those who have consciously used religion
for material ends have often come to be affected much more
deeply, as any wise priest well knows.

But in the history of religion we encounter this sort of
religious aspiration as by far the commonest type, and in
passing it may be noted that it has itself great psychothera-
peutic value. We are stabilized in our emotions when we
come to feel that we are not helpless in a hostile universe,
but that we can do something to control our destinies, so
that, insofar as religion increases our hopes for crops and
income or success in examinations, it quiets psychological
unrest and so increases man's power and happiness. James

was only telling the experience of the ages when he advised the new Christians to "pray for one another that ye may be healed. The effectual fervent prayer of a righteous man availeth much." The miracles of healing in the early church show that it was not only spiritual illness which the saint had in mind.

Where religion that seeks objective goods leaves off and the type that looks directly for subjective improvement begins it is hard to say. Few religious people have no objective aspirations. However strongly we believe that we should not seek objective goods in religion, not many people could resist praying or asking a priest or minister to pray for the recovery of a desperately ill little daughter. But we are in quite a new type of religion when we begin to look primarily for a means of healing our own distraught personalities. I do not think that this is the contrast Tillich intended when he distinguished magic from religion, though this is in a real sense also a use of religion for personal benefit. But religion practiced for subjective rather than objective good clearly presents an important contrast, however mixed the two may usually appear in an individual. In what follows, however, we shall limit the discussion to those types of experience that, consciously or unconsciously, aim at subjective good.

Further, I do not intend to discuss religion in the sense in which most sociologists and anthropologists consider it, namely, as a social institution. It seems that religion in this sense is a collective residuum of individual experiences and that religion in this collective form has power only insofar as it can impress itself anew, relive itself, in the fresh experiences of each generation. In most societies—by no means all—this collective residuum of individual experience has long since been captured and capitalized on by an organized priesthood, which is itself a social factor of the greatest importance. Our interest will be in the religion of the individual, and so we shall deal with religion in its socialized sense only from the point of view of the individual, who, presented with it as part of his tradition, usually (if he is a good churchman) builds a replica of its demands within himself.

Freudian readers will find it conspicuous that, though my psychological formulation owes much to Freud, I have offered no such rigid scheme of the psyche's infantile development as did the master. I do not say that the Freudians are wrong in their scheme, but I do say that they will not have established their case until they do not require us to give up our "resistance" to be convinced. The basic conceptions that the child's psychic development follows an invariable sequence and that the individual character is totally the product of his experiences seem to geneticists incredible. Julian Huxley recently addressed a conference of psychologists in London and, according to *The Times* of London, said that they would have to give up these conceptions as quite wrong. Far from the psyche's being a *tabula rasa* at birth, on which social experiences make their formative impressions, it is widely known that the gene formation of human beings differs more widely from individual to individual than is true of any other animal. No one disputes that individuals vary in intelligence or that some are born tone deaf or color blind. The social environment did not make Shakespeare into Shakespeare or Bach into Bach in creative ability. There is as little reason to suppose that social sensitivity as against callousness, shyness as against boldness, passion as against coldness—much as these develop and express themselves in social relations—are the product of those relations. I can only register my doubts here, but without training in the field I cannot hope or try to solve the problems such a statement evokes.

Religion does, however, have some light to throw on the so-called Oedipus problem. In its baldly literal form, the Oedipus concept is a notion that every little boy finds his greatest problem of adjustment to life in his relation to his father. To this I agree, at least for boys in our civilization. The father does, of course, usually present to the boy his chief rival for the mother's affections, affections which he passionately wants to monopolize. The older siblings or the coming of a new baby to "break his nose" also present the two- or three-year-old with real problems. His id wants the mother entirely for himself. All these rivalries, especially that with the father, leave their mark. Some boys "master" the problem with apparently relative ease, whereas others are marred by the conflict all their lives.

In Freudian terms, however, the problem becomes much more specific, namely, that the boy's desire is to take the father's place in actually copulating with the mother. The superego condemns him for the desire, and "as a rule," Freud says, the mother tells him that the father is so angry with him that he plans to castrate the little fellow. Whether the mother says this or not, the boy wants to kill the father, both to have free access to the mother and to escape the terrible penalty that he feels his father wishes to visit on him. This tension, it is asserted, usually reaches its height when the boy is three years old, and thereafter its elements —that is, the desire for the mother, the fear of the father, and the desire to kill him—are slowly but thoroughly repressed. But, even when repressed, the problem emerges from the unconscious in all sorts of apparently irrelevant associations as a sense of guilt. When a neurotic patient is analyzed by a Freudian, it almost universally turns out that his guilt or its concomitant, his sense of inferiority, arises from or expresses itself in a sexual problem or a problem with the parents, one that can be resolved only as the patient can be led to recall the original guilt and fear he associated with sex as he first experienced it in the father–mother–child complication.[2] Those who "master" the Oedipus complex in childhood presumably become what James called the "healthy minded." His patients were, however, the guilt-ridden neurotics whose lives had been perverted by not mastering the Oedipus complex, and these, roughly, would have been James's "sick souls."

The residual guilt in such an adult, Freudians continue, must be appeased by punishment. So man tortures himself in various ways, for example, by frigidity; by homosexuality, that is, sex in which a woman (the mother) is not involved; or by ability to perform only with women he despises, like prostitutes, because he cannot "sully" a woman he admires. There are scores of such ways of appeasing or escaping the sense of guilt. A more healthy adult revolts from the father and so kills at least the father's dominance within him. Another solution, of course, is to let the father spiritually castrate him by obeying his every command, going into the father's business, until the boy really loses his own personality and becomes a replica of the father. In such a case, he can regain his self-respect, as Fromm pointed out, only by absorbing in turn the personalities of his own sons

[2] Freud stated this theory most succinctly in his last book, *An Outline of Psychoanalysis* (New York: 1949), pp. 90–99. He first announced it in one of his early books, *The Interpretation of Dreams* (New York: Basic Books, 1955). In his essay, "Transformations of Puberty," written some years later, Freud said that recognition of the Oedipus complex, whose mastery is the task of every human being, "has become the shibboleth that distinguishes the adherents of psycho-analysis from its opponents." (*Three Essays on the Theory of Sexuality* [New York: Basic Books, 1962], p. 92 n.) Freud believed that "he that is not with me is against me," and "with me" always implied acceptance of every detail of his thought.

78

or inferiors. The guilt would only be fully assuaged as a son allows the father to kill him outright. Such, at least, would be the logical outcome of the Oedipus complex.

It is at this point that the salvation from guilt offered by religion comes to mind. Strangely, it has not been remarked that the great source of forgiveness, of freedom from guilt, of reconciliation with the father, has taken on much of the same pattern in the Jewish-Christian tradition, especially in Christian ideas of salvation which go back to Paul and John. The subject can only be opened here.

According to Genesis, the innocence of Adam and Eve consisted in their sexual ignorance. Milton to the contrary, there is no hint in the Bible that the two had sexual relations while they were in the Garden. Then they ate the fruit of the forbidden tree of knowledge of good and evil, and it was this "first disobedience" that God punished by expelling them from Eden. But, so far as knowledge of good and evil went, the only thing they learned, and learned instantly from the eating, was the shame of exposing their sexual parts even to a spouse. These they had at once to cover with leaves. With no such direct connection in the story, their new knowledge apparently also included how to use them, since they at once began begetting children after their expulsion. Good and evil, that is, seem in the story to have been sexual matters, with exposure specifically an evil.

Jews who are orthodox have ever since continued the sense of shame in exposure. The Greek *gymnasium*, by its very name a place of naked exercising, was introduced once in Jewish history, but to the utter scandal of all Jewish tradition, and was rejected as soon as orthodoxy could reassert itself. Today Jews are proud that they have no such tradition of condemning sex as have the Christians, but an orthodox Jew, although he honors sex and is required to "multiply," may have intercourse only with his wife and only with her in the dark. So, when the ancient psalmist exclaims, "In sin did my mother conceive me," [3] I believe that he is expressing much more of the Jewish attitude than Jews generally like to admit. It must never be forgotten that Freud and by far the greater number of his followers spoke from a Jewish, not a Christian, background. With Philo, so far as I know, the attitude that sex is associated with sin and guilt was first made explicit in Judaism, but he did this under Greek influence, and to understand him we must look at Greek tradition.

In spite of the Greek freedom about nakedness and sexual practices, they were Greeks who first made the flesh the inherent center and source of human sin and the soul an immaterial divine presence. The early Greeks could have their gods cavort in sexual delights and use phallic symbols and figures for their deepest religious aspirations. But Plato probably spoke also for the Pythagoreans when he wanted these stories taken out of children's education and made the old Orphic contrast of body and spirit chiefly a struggle with the degrading power of lust. After Plato, it was a commonplace to make sexual continence the price of spiritual attainment. If the old sexual symbols and language were still used, they were made into the language of union with the divine female principle or into replacing the divine creative masculine—that is, it became the language of mysticism, as it did in the biblical Song of Songs.

With Philo, these two came together, and Abraham's relation with Sarah represented the mystical begetting of a divine baby. Philo made much of the biblical verse[4] which says that Isaac, in taking Rebekah as his wife, took her into the tent of his mother to have intercourse with her and thereby was comforted for his mother's death. Philo did not

[3] Ps. 51:5.
[4] Gen. 24:67.

80

call the serpent of Eden the phallus, indeed, but he made it the symbol of sexual pleasure, so that no one can doubt that for him, as for Plato, the sin and guilt of man are basically matters of sex. Philo would have every man solve the problem in the Greek way, that of allowing intercourse only for the begetting of children, and he regarded it as otherwise utterly corrupting. Instead of the sexual act, he wanted a mystical eros with God and *sophia*. This, he said, was true Judaism.

Jews have revived such a mystical Judaism repeatedly through the centuries, but the mainstream of Judaism since the Middle Ages has solved its guilt problem by obeying the law of God. It accepted the fatherhood of God to the point that complete and detailed obedience to the law was the whole duty of man, his way of achieving the height of Jewish piety, "the imitation of God," what we saw was one of the solutions of the Oedipus complex. Jews have long taken God everywhere into their lives by having a divine law that would tell how each thing should be done. Jews recognize but one sacrament, the sacrament of obedience. And yet, on the High Holy Days, when they most try to appease the sense of guilt which still haunts them since they know they have not fulfilled their obligations perfectly, the great symbolic story for Jewish hope is that of what they call the Akedah, "the binding," that is, the story of Abraham's sacrificing Isaac. The sacrifice was stopped, in the biblical story, and a ram supplied by divine intervention to take Isaac's place. The rabbis later expanded the story in many ways. Isaac, the willing victim, according to one account, carried the wood on his shoulder as one carries a cross, and the story goes on to assure us that, at the climax, when the angel of God has Abraham substitute the ram for Isaac, the substitution by no means replaced Isaac, for it was Isaac himself who was sacrificed and who rose from the dead. The sho-

phar, a ram's horn, is accordingly blown in the ritual to recall this sacrifice, so that God as he hears it will move from
the seat of justice to the seat of mercy and will forgive.
Guilt is removed when God recalls the father who at his
command really did kill his son. Since God commanded it,
it was God who killed the boy or the ram in his place and
whose judgment against mankind is replaced by mercy and
forgiveness when the shophar sounds. The tradition is very
complex, and I have analyzed it in detail in Volume Four
of my *Jewish Symbols*,[5] so that I need not expand on it
here.[6]

If, however, traditional Judaism only suggested that man's
guilt is removed by a father who killed his son, the great
tradition of Christianity made this motif absolutely central.
The early Christians liked to depict their own salvation
through Christ by the figure of Abraham sacrificing Isaac,
but that idea was much more deeply developed from the
very beginning in explaining the significance of the death
of Christ. Adopting from hellenized Judaism the Greek
notion that the material world and the human body are sinful, our earliest Christian sources proclaim that men can lose
their sin and guilt at the cross. God, it seems, could be rec-

[5] New Haven: Yale University Press, 1954.
[6] As an example of the indirect method of using evidence, I may cite
the essay of Theodor Reik, "The Shofar (the Ram's Horn)," in his
Ritual, Psycho-analytic Studies (New York: 1946), pp. 221–361. Reik
discussed the simple and direct story of Abraham's readiness to sacrifice
the boy at God's command, but turned it so completely around that at
the end he made it a witness for the Oedipus complex on the ground that
the story was really telling of Isaac's desire to kill his father. Erich Fromm
has recently republished his essay arguing that "adoptionism" was the
Christology of the first centuries of Christianity, that it represented the
Oedipal desire to displace the father, and that this faded out only as
the social condition of the Christian group rose "two or three centuries
later." His interpretation seems to me inadequate equally from the historical and psychological points of view. See his *The Dogma of Christ*
(New York: 1963), pp. 1–91.

onciled with sinful (fleshly) men only by the death of his son. God so loved the world that he sent his only son to perish in it, so that whoever believes in him might not perish but have eternal life, that the world (that is, sinful men) might be saved through him, and he who believes in him is no longer condemned.[7] In Freudian language, man through Christ loses his feeling that he is condemned by the father because the sense of guilt is removed.

Paul also taught that man loses his sense of guilt or condemnation through the death of Christ. But, according to both Paul and John, a man can be thus freed of guilt only as he becomes identified with the crucified son. John talks of the necessity of a new birth, not of the flesh, but of the spirit, that is, without material defilement,[8] but he also lays great stress on our eating Christ's flesh and drinking his blood.[9] Paul could escape his guilt only as he "became a new creature in Christ Jesus," [10] which he achieved as he died with Christ in baptism and rose from the dead with him.[11] For God was in Christ reconciling the world to himself.[12] As our old (material) self is crucified with Christ and we rise into a "newness of life," we do so without guilt; when our sinful body is thus destroyed, we are freed from sin, since one who has died is free from sin. As dead to sin, we are alive to God.[13] The conflict of the higher mind and the bodily mind within man of which I spoke in the preceding chapter is ended, and this body, which produces only sin and guilt, is removed. "For God . . . sending his son in the likeness of sinful flesh and for sin, condemned sin in the

[7] John 3:16–18.
[8] John 3:1–12.
[9] John 6:25–59.
[10] II Cor. 5:17.
[11] Rom. 6:1–4.
[12] II Cor. 5:18 f.
[13] Rom. 6:6–11.

flesh . . . so that we walk not according to the flesh but the spirit." [14] So all guilt, condemnation, is removed collectively because the Son was killed; and individually, as we are killed with the Son, we come into a new life without condemnation, because we are reconciled with the Father.

The symbol of this release from guilt is the crucifix, the son being killed, but the symbol of the goal we achieve is that of the single baby eternally happy in his mother's arms. Cherubs may fly about, God the father may be represented above, but he smiles in satisfaction as the baby usurps the mother's lap and breast. I have asked many men about their sense of identification as they looked as such an icon and have invariably been answered that they identify with the baby. His peace and triumph become theirs. Women, on the contrary, say they identify with the mother, which opens another door that we shall not try to enter here. The church never allows us to forget that the price of such triumphant peace was the death of the son, sent out to his death by the father, though a willing victim of sacrifice.

That is, the Christian message of hope is that we can indeed be freed from fleshly guilt, not by killing the father, but by the father's killing us in our individual assertiveness and raising us into a new life of identity with the son who is now restored as one with the father and completely at home with the mother, the Queen of Heaven. It is not in point here to trace the history of this in Christian theology. I believe that the Catholics are right in saying that the experience of redemption was almost at once, if not quite from the beginning, mediated to the faithful in the sacraments of baptism, penance, and the Eucharist. It was several centuries before Christianity fully adopted the Virgin and Child as the symbol of final achievement, and the doctrine of her perpetual virginity, apparently unknown to the

[14] Rom. 8:1–12.

evangelists, also developed later. The development was only a logical conclusion to the earlier assumptions, however, since, in the perfect life without body or sin, fleshly intercourse has no place whatever.

What are we saying, that Christian theories of guilt and its removal confirm the Freudian theory of Oedipus? As Freud considered the actual problems of the three-year-old boy, certainly not. One would indeed have to project an *idée fixe* to find any suggestion of castration in the story of Christian redemption. I can myself take neither theory literally. It seems to me little more than a symbolic myth that there is actually a God who reconciled himself to men for their fleshly sin and disobedience by sending his only son to be crucified. Similarly, I cannot believe that every three-year-old boy actually wants to kill his father to have free sexual relations with his mother. Both, however, seem to indicate that, at least in our Greco-Jewish civilization of censured sex, we must live in conflict and guilt if we are sensitive people and that the only hope of freedom from that guilt lies in such a fresh orientation to some great reality of which we are parts, one which, following the pattern of childhood, both Freud and the early Christians symbolically regarded as a father.

Something still deeper, however, seems to be involved. The problem may well lie in the fact that the little lusty and lusting id must be cut back, restrained, civilized, become acceptable to humanity, that is, acceptable to the father. Freud said that the id wants to kill the father and go its own way, whereas theology says that the only solution is for the father to kill the id, at least in its self-assertion, and bring it or us into an entirely new kind of life. In terms of the two myths, Freud seems to have described the problem better, theology to have solved it better. That is, theology has better shown the way to peace of mind and freedom from guilt. The immediate problem is a personal, not a racial one. We inherit, not the sin and guilt of Adam, but the nature of Adam, which must assert itself in revolt against authority. The id's essential character is this assertiveness. Peace lies in our giving it over and conforming to the universal.

At this point, we see that, not only are Christianity and the Greco-Jewish traditions involved, but also the religious patterns of the East, in which the great sin men commit is essentially in being individuals at all. By these patterns, we can have real peace only as we return to the universal. Anaximander almost alone of the Greeks recognized this. Theophrastus reports him as saying:

> And into that from which things take their rise they pass away once more, "as is meet; for they make reparation and satisfaction to one another for their injustice according to the ordering of time," as he says in these somewhat poetical terms.[15]

To Theophrastus, this was poetic fancy, but not to the millions of pious Hindus and Buddhists, who see the emergence of the individual man, like that of the individual oak or mountain, as a phenomenon that nature must eradicate by reabsorbing it.

Christianity never went so far as did the Eastern pandits and always looked for the perpetuation of the individual— but not of the individual id. There had been that sort of thing once in heaven, but God had condemned all its exponents, the fallen angels, to hell. Freud, as many good Christians have suspected, belonged with those fallen ones, because, quite without thinking it through in such terms, they have felt that his myth glorified and perpetuated the

[15] The fragment is quoted as cited and translated by John Burnet, *Early Greek Philosophy* (London: 1920), p. 52.

id that could come fully into its own only as it rid itself in one way or another of the incubus of the father.

In this, more deeply than he himself suspected, Freud spoke for the new age, spoke in a mythology which belonged with Nietzsche's superman. The impulses of modern scientists, of the newly evolving nations, of our rebellious adolescents, follow the pattern of Freud, not of Christianity. Modern thinkers seek personal fulfillment, ask the father to disappear or adjust to the fact that they are going to assert themselves; they ask new questions, flout conventions. That way lies exhilaration, but no peace. Today we need a far deeper kind of cooperation or socialization than the past has ever known, with its alternating between wars and sacraments, guilt and atonement. We must somehow find a Greek middle ground between the Nietzschean-Freudian personal assertion and what they considered the Jewish-Christian solution of submission, slavery, death. It is a problem that we can hope to solve only as we better understand both religion and psychology—better understand that we are and must be individuals, but that at the same time we are a part of humanity and of nature.

4

Types of
Religious Experience

BEFORE ENUMERATING AND DISCUSSING distinct types of religious experience, it should be emphasized that the types are themselves only abstractions, convenient categories of description, and that no individual will ever present himself as a pure type. The same is true of every traditional religion, for in all of them almost every type of experience can be found. The difference between a "great religion" or a "church" and a sect is that the former usually offers stimuli for every type of experience, so that people of all sorts can find satisfaction in it or several kinds of satisfaction; the sect tries to restrict itself to a single type, but usually can do so for only a short while, since, as it grows larger, it will have to appeal to a greater variety of people. One type will normally predominate in an individual's life; but he will certainly show the active influence of several others. This will be taken for granted by those who are used to thinking in terms of psychological or psychopathic types, since all classifications of neuroses or psychoses are suggestive, rather than specific or exclusive.

Legalism

The first type of religious experience to consider is what I call "legalism." Every man in every society is born into an environment of rigorous rules. From infancy with his mother-father and siblings, even with larger social impacts, the child develops his social orientation by absorbing the rules of society as part of himself. Some he learns consciously; others he acquires by unconscious imitation. In a simple society, the rules are such that a child can learn them adequately as he grows up among his fellow tribesman. But all advanced societies and most savage societies have developed elaborate rules, taboos, folkways with no approximation to a system, so that many of the rules contradict one another. This conflict lies at the root of much of Greek tragedy. Even if he could understand and reconcile them, the individual, especially a punctilious individual, finds them too diverse. To his utter confusion, he discovers that he is constantly breaking laws unawares or that he is unable to control the id because a confused socialization is a weak one. Or he must make choices and decisions and cannot tell which is the "right" one to make.

Legalism is a type of religion directed primarily to solving this problem. The good man, legalism tells us, can do what is right if he knows what is right, and he will know the right, not by a personal intuition or revelation or by deciding the merits of a situation for himself, but from a code that tells him exactly what to do at every point. Legalism is a religion in which a man takes a code of laws or customs, written or unwritten, as the unquestioned authority and has a sense of right-doing or of guilt according as he does or does not follow the requirements of this code. To have force, the code of legalism can never be one's own creation. It must present in definite form the guiding principles of a group, class, tribe, or civilization. Or of God. It must be a curtain on which the right is spelled out for us in terms comprehensible and specific. The security it offers stems precisely from this fact, that through its observance a man becomes an acceptable member of the larger group, human or divine.

It can at once be objected that all I am describing is the normal process of the socialization of the individual by which the standards and requirements of the parents are built into him and these standards and requirements enlarged by further contact with his fellows. Indeed, we might abandon this whole process to the sociologist or to the secularists of whatever name who want to keep themselves free of religious terminology, if to do so would not rule out some of the most important religions of the world. Judaism and Brahmanism, for example, specifically state that the observance of their requirements is the basic element of their religious structures. Jews like to say that their religion is based on "orthoproxy," doing the right thing, rather than "orthodoxy," holding the right ideas. From this we go on to other religions and see, not only that Catholicism has a definite code of conduct, one which it would indignantly refuse to call irrelevant to its religion, but that Protestantism, at least in its typical early stages, was strictly

puritanical. Even the Church of England, for all its elastic-
ity, upholds the English Sunday and in the name of religion
kept Princess Margaret from doing "wrong" by marrying
a man whose wife had left him for another. All of this (and
a thousand things more) is legalism and religion at the same
time. Those who want to distinguish religious from secular
life forget that, through most of the past and in the great
majority of civilizations today, man never has had the first
inkling that the laws of his society were anything but
sacred.

Even the Greeks, prime exhibit of secularism, believed
that all their basic laws had such divine sanction that to
break them brought upon men the vengeance of the Furies.
And the primary laws of the Greeks, thus guaranteed by
divine sanction, included the incest taboo, adultery, the
rights of strangers to hospitality, and (the ancestor of all
banking laws) the inviolability of money or goods left with
a friend for safekeeping during a journey. It is quite too
large a matter to be rehearsed here, but the Greeks in their
various cities lived by codes of laws which seemed to them
quite as sacred as the laws of Moses did to the Jews. Indeed,
they also looked back in Sparta to a half-divine Lycurgus,
in Crete to a similar Minos and Rhadamanthus, who were
semidivine legislators of what we regard as "secular" laws.
The Greeks thought that these same men would be their
judges in the afterlife. And Solon tells us explicitly that his
codification of Athenian law was made to bring divine right
or justice into the lives of men. No Jew could say more of
Moses or of his law.

Early Roman law had similar beginnings in laws that they
called *fas, ius,* and the *boni mores,* all of which harked back
to a divine origin or sanction. The Roman declaration, *vox
populi vox dei* ("The voice of the people is the voice of
God") continued to guarantee that Roman legislation had

divine sanction, although at various periods the "voice of the people" was thought to be pronounced in very different ways.

It is not in point here to trace the almost universal assumption in Western civilizations and indeed throughout the world that the laws by which men live have a divine origin. Throughout the Middle Ages, men thought that the law of the state had a thoroughly subservient and relative value as compared to the law of God presented by the Church. The result was that the modern state could at the outset free itself of ecclesiastical control only by setting up a divine origin for itself in a king who himself ruled by "divine right." When people looked for a more democratic origin of law, they turned toward the "natural" or "divine" right, still implicitly the basic law of our own country. The attempt in France and America to secularize laws only meant their freeing from priestly control, not their reduction to the sanction of passing opinion. *Vox populi* again became *vox dei*.

Still the vast majority of men think of their laws, not as a pragmatic convenience, but as a statement of "right." Similarly, our ethical conventions, many of which are firmly protected by statute or court decisions, resemble what the Romans called their "good customs" in that, within our own borders at least, we consider them indisputably right. Our laws prohibit "sex crimes," felonious assault, perjury, robbery, murder, and breach of trust, to name only a few, and these we do not regard as human conveniences but as so right that no religious-minded person could commit them. Every minister and priest regards breach of them as not only civil crime, but as religious sin, and our society as a whole fully agrees.

Some laws are only religious laws, like the Catholic prohibition of meat on Friday or the Jewish kosher laws. In modern times, the state has increasingly tried to secularize the laws of marriage and divorce, but in the popular mind and in most courts marriage still has its religious character, confused as most people are as to how the right in such matters should be defined. But in this and in general, secular and religious laws blend so indistinguishably together that the legal structure of a society becomes one of the most important elements in the religion of a society. The rabbis taught this when they laid down one of the chief principles of rabbinic Judaism: "The law of the land is Law." That is, Law, the Torah, the holy law of the Jews, includes the laws of whichever nation a Jew may be living in. An observant Jew considers that his duty to pay taxes, to serve on the jury, to vote at elections, and all the rest are part of his legal obligation to God, of his religion.

Protestantism, both Lutheran and Calvinist, similarly divided religion itself into the law and the gospel. To Lutherans, the rulers were "ordained by God," and their laws had divine authority unless they contravened moral or ecclesiastical doctrine. Then the leaders of the church would beg the ruler to change his laws, or, if necessary, they would passively resist to the point of martyrdom. But the law of the state had divine sanction and occupied a most important place in their religion. The Calvinists knew no passive resistance. In the name of God, they were quite prepared to take over the state, and, if they could not themselves become legislators, they proposed to see to it that the rulers made and enforced the "right" laws. The Catholic Church has never really accepted the secular state at all, as their control of legislation in Catholic countries shows. The pope has the ultimate word for all men, not only in faith, but in morals, and to Catholics his moral pronouncements are law. Religion and morality are quite synonymous terms to the vast majority of our people.

Legalism is a religion based on specific definitions. As the law of the land must tell us clearly what we may and may not do, so religious legalism brings its comfort only when it is specific. When I was a devout Methodist boy, my parents put up a large motto in my room: "What would Jesus do?" This meant, in practice, that I should feel terribly guilty if I did not follow the strictest requirements of our puritanical code, in the privacy of my own bedroom first of all. Rarely, indeed, did any doubt or debate arise, for Jesus would infallibly obey the wishes, live by the standards of, his parents. I must do the same by my parents. The strength of the appeal lay in its direct intelligibility. When I had been to church five times of a Sunday and read only religious literature between services, I could go to bed in a contented frame of mind. If you wish to call it a self-righteous frame of mind, I do not object. The function of the legalism was to define exactly what divine and human society demanded of me and hence to give me security and inner peace as I complied and controlled my id. When I grew older, the simplicity of this situation disappeared.

Precisely when we think that we have put legalism down, it re-emerges in greater strength. For example, the extreme form of Protestant revolt against salvation by legal conformity emerged in Calvinism. The pious Puritan, stripped of every symbolic act or object, faced the bare walls of his meetinghouse bereft theoretically also of every comfort of legalism. Having done all, he counted himself a worm in God's sight, whose only hope would be in an act of God, never in any effort to conform to God's will which he might make. He was taught that he would never know in this life whether he was one of the elect, pleasing to God; and he should so magnify the glory of God as to become indifferent to his own fate. "Will you praise God eternally in hell-fire if you are not one of the elect?" or, "Are you willing to be damned for the glory of God?" were old questions asked in Presbyterian ordination, and to such a disregard of self in the glory of God all Calvinists were supposed to come. Calvinism expected a man to live in the social environment of that terrifying God, assured that his most frantic efforts to conform to that environment would have no effect at the end. It was too much to expect of human nature. So the very sects which most completely disavowed any hope of earning God's favor became the most active legalists of them all. Quite unconsciously, they turned the circle and came back to the most elemental stage of taboo and censoriousness. The satisfaction of doing God's will, of pleasing God, which they denied themselves in theory, the sense of adjustment with God which by their theology they should never have felt, came to them, bless their hearts, through the back door in the form of the Blue Laws.

Legalism has its full value as a religious pattern only in unified societies, which offer no divergencies or contradictory codes. The joy of traditional Judaism (and joy it is) can be felt only in a Jewish community living in collective observance, for only so does the law present itself without complications as really the formulation of one's social center. Jews who lived in "Jewish quarters" in Alexandria long before the Christian era did so by choice, so that together they could live the life of the law. Christians have done terrible things to Jews in the ghettos, but Jews themselves created the ghettos, if not the locks on them. The only disagreement was about who was to have the key. Jews of old wanted to live together because the benefit and peace of legalism can come only when men are faced with a single code, unchallenged by rival codes.

Every community that wants happiness in living by a code must do the same. British gentlemen could be as intransigent as extreme Jews and wear their dinner jackets in the tropics, like an orthodox Jew wearing his yarmalka when studying in the Yale Library. But the code of a gentleman brings its satisfaction chiefly in association with other gentlemen who do not challenge the niceties. Gentlemen tend just as much as Jews to form their own ghettos, by creating retreats from those not living by the gentleman's code; they like "proper" home addresses, schools, and clubs. George Apley, who sold his house when he saw his neighbor across the street sitting on his veranda in shirtsleeves, was fleeing to a ghetto safe for a Boston Brahman.

In this way, legalism produces the caste or group. "A born gentleman" is psychologically one who is born of "chosen people," the "right" people. Each group, the one with its written code and the other with its unwritten code, believes that it constitutes a special bloc, where in-group marriage is one of the basic demands. If an orthodox (and many an unorthodox) Jew would be horrified at his son's proposing to marry a gentile, the necessity of those living by the code of the gentry to marry only their own kind binds just as tightly, as both George Apley and the Irish Catholic father of his fiancée frankly recognized. A son of mine heard one of his classmates at a private school remark to another classmate: "You can't go around with that girl, Jim; her parents aren't in the Social Register!"

The upper castes of India have essentially the same life, and again can keep themselves true to the laws of their castes, can find the relaxation and security of their caste, only by the same exclusive associations. The Samurai class in Japan was also marked off as the group born to a definite code. It would be only a matter of research and tabulation to show how elaborately the Brahman, the Confucian, the Parsi have made their religions into not only legal structures, but exclusive social structures.

To live by the rule of monasticism, monks must similarly withdraw from the rest of society, even from the daily life of the ordinary priest. In the life of the monk, three things are required—poverty, chastity, and obedience, but the greatest of these is obedience, since obedience underlies both the others. The monastery, that is, offers another ghetto where the life of the law can be lived in tranquillity. Its inmates are called "regulars" because they live by the *regulae*, the laws. The tranquillity of monastic life shows legalism in its perfection. The social urge is fully codified in the rule of the order, and moral problems no longer exist. If one has the "gift of chastity" and so can endure the life physiologically, probably no form of living is so peaceful.

Most of us, however, are not Brahmans in either the Indian or the Boston sense, are not orthodox Jews or self-isolated gentlemen or monks. The full power of religious legalism cannot satisfy us because, in modern complicated society, each aspect of life presents us with a different code. This I found as I emerged from boyhood and the motto, "What would Jesus do?" no longer simply meant that I should live by the puritanical legalism of my parents.

In more complex societies, the individual is presented with a variety of mores. Take the problem of a Jew in America, for example. His own people, organized as Orthodox, Conservative, and Reform (with a "right" and "left" in each group), present him with several quite distinct approaches to proper conduct. In addition, he is given the codes of American business, of sportsmanship, and of the gentleman. Most Jews take one of the Jewish codes along with a gentile code simultaneously and thereby actually come into what we have seen is basically polytheism, since an entirely different right stands behind each as its ultimate guarantee. This bifurcation has been movingly described by Maurice Samuel in his *The Gentleman and the Jew.*

From his utterly simple home of Rumanian Jewry, he went
to an English school and read the English boys' books,
where the sportsman's ideals of the clean fight were presented as the mores. He saw in Kipling and Shakespeare
the gentleman's code carried out into a philosophy of im-
perialism.

> "A good clean fight, no hitting below the belt, may the best
> man win, and no hard feelings": on the battlefield as in the
> ring. One could put these words accurately into Yiddish,
> but they would be gibberish. Jews looked on all fighting,
> private and public, personal and historic, as such a disgust-
> ing business that they could not associate it with an affirma-
> tive code; and I felt this so strongly even in my boyhood
> that I despaired of ever giving my parents a glimpse into
> the sunny combativeness of the St. Jim's *Weltanschauung.*
> How could I begin to reconcile it with the somber
> thoughtfulness of the Pentateuch and *The Ethics of the
> Fathers?* Where, within that subtle and perceptive disci-
> pline, could you find room for the dashing buccaneer type,
> who could make his prisoners walk the plank, but who,
> beneath everything, was something of a gentleman because
> he knew the meaning of "a fair fight"? And in what terms
> could I present to my *Rebbi* the honorable features in the
> characters of a Captain Kidd and Claude Duval? [1]

For a time, Samuel thought it clear that the gentile ideal
was that of the sportsman, the Jewish ideal, that of the man
who fought only when he could do nothing else, but who
always considered it, when pushed on him, a departure
from all that was ideal or fine. Samuel had the two beautifully distinguished until, as a boy, he went to an English
church and heard the vicar preach, in the name of Jesus,

[1] Maurice Samuel, *The Gentleman and the Jew* (New York: 1950), p.
31.

exactly the ideas of long-suffering and avoidance of conflict that he had learned from his rebbi and parents. His distinctions gone Samuel faced the tremendum. He describes how, after much travail of soul, he came to reject the gentleman's mores for those of the Jew, though he still so often engages in controversy that it is difficult to believe he does not enjoy a fight.

If we are in business, we have an additional code, that of "business ethics," where neither gentlemanly sportsmanship nor the Jewish-Christian kindness have traditionally intruded at all. If the right behind business ethics were personalized and represented in a statue, it would have a totally different countenance and pose from the statues of either Jesus or the god of sport. Many a businessman has rebuked his rector for a sermon which seemed to impose Christian ethics on the business world. And one of the chief synagogues in New York long had the custom of requiring the rabbi to submit in advance the manuscript of his sermon to a committee of several businessmen in the congregation to make sure that Jewis ethics were not made to intrude on business ethics. This was not to guarantee the purity of Jewish religion, but to allow the members of the congregation to worship Mammon along with Yahweh, to do so by following the laws set by each.

It seems a safe guess that the minister or rabbi in a fashionable church or synagogue who ignored the major points of the code of a gentleman would be even more quickly out of favor, if not dismissed, than if he had liberal economic ideas. Actually, the code of a gentleman can be as sufficient a religious approach to life as either of the other two. The code of a gentleman is difficult to discuss because, like the code of business, it has never been codified. No one could do so without making himself ridiculous. Indeed, it will be considered bad taste for me even to bring up the matter thus directly, for one of the basic laws of the gentleman is that he doesn't discuss the subject. Yet the gentleman must be able to recognize and snub a "bounder" on the street or in the drawing room with the skill that in his earlier days he showed in cricket or fencing. There is much in the gentleman that Samuel missed, notably the sense of *noblesse oblige* toward those so far beneath one as to be in no sense rivals. But to grind one's tenants and refuse them charity has never been so direct a disqualification of a gentleman as to be caught cheating at cards in a gentlemen's club or doing anything else "caddish" with other gentleman or ladies. Lord Chesterfield, the arch-gentleman and arch-villain of them all, found all this an entirely adequate religion by which to live and die. He is reported to have said on his deathbed that he had no fear of meeting God at the final judgment, for he was sure God was a gentleman who would recognize another gentleman when he saw one. A religion that makes people thus confident in the face of both life and death is a real religion, whether it is a religion we admire or not.

I have no interest in evaluating these various codes; I am only trying at the moment to show that legalism is a basic and, at least in part, an inevitable form of religion and that what makes it so is not the origin or value of a given code but how the individual regards it. Whether a code was written down by Moses, Lycurgus, Zarathustra, Emily Post, or has never been written at all does not matter for our discussion. The religion of legalism is the acceptance of any code as embodying "the right," "the good customs," and taking that code as an absolute guide for conduct, an active and actual curtain from the tremendum. It becomes a religious experience when, by a sense of having obeyed and conformed, one gets a sense of inner rightness and external security with man and with "the right" or God. Psychologically, legalism makes life more peaceful within and more secure without because it resolves the confusion and uncertainty of the demands of both human and divine society.

Some element of legalism is a necessity of human nature. We mentioned the fact that not only law is necessary for society, but laws on certain universal human problems. The nature of man is such that his very existence requires a legal structure for his society and himself. It is a law of human nature that man, individually and as a group, must have a code by which to live.

At the basic level of man to which I am trying to direct the reader, our departmental and categorical divisions disappear. Religion, the life of acceptance and devotion, functions clearly in our devotion to a given structure of conduct.

Why, then, if the religion of legalism is thus universal and inescapable, do some religious people so often denounce it, as Paul Tillich has said: "That is not religion; it is legalism"? The first answer is that Tillich is looking to what seem to him higher approaches to the life of devotion than legalism offers. He would be the first to admit that he is committed to standards of conduct for himself and distressed at gross departures from them in himself (if ever) and in others. There are many other approaches to religion, other types of religious experience, than legalism. I have discussed it first because it is the most common single type. Tillich contrasts it with religion, actually, only to emphasize what he considers a more noble and true approach to reality than that of following a traditional code. I agree with him entirely that other types of religious adjustment have a more ennobling and inspiring effect. But to deny that legalism has any place in religion at all is to deny one of the facts of life, for legalism works in all of us and is not only the whole religion of a large part of mankind, but is most of the religion of most of us.

In discussing the types of religious experience, we shall repeatedly have to close by pointing out their dangers and possible perversions. Every type of religious experience comes to a bad end when carried to its logical conclusion. The tragic end of legalism has throughout been hinted in what has been said; it can bring one into intolerant smugness, a self-righteousness which Jesus, rightly or wrongly, taught us to call pharisaism. The traditional fault of the Pharisees consisted not so much in their hypocrisy as in their being what Jesus called, "whole, in no need of a physician," the people whom William James treated with only slightly veiled sarcasm as "the healthy-minded." To know with ultimate confidence that you are living the right life and that those who do otherwise are common, vulgar, pagan, impure, wordly—whatever may be your term for the nonconformist—indicates spiritual death. In a world where mankind really does not know what is right, these men live in certainty. They may be the dogmatic conservatives or the dogmatic radicals, both of whose harshness of speech and truculence always amazes the man in the middle of the road groping along without a rope at either side to guide him. These people have found peace and security, but at the price, Jesus believed, of spiritual degradation.

Jesus, accordingly, like many, took another path. Much as we must all in large part be legalists, I fully agree with Jesus about the dangers of legalism as a dominant pattern.

Supralegalism

Above or beyond legalism is quite a different pattern of religion which still has its central concern in conduct. In "supralegalism," one bursts through the socially provided curtain, at least on some points, to fresh perceptions and judgments for oneself. What should I do to inherit eternal life? the rich young man asked Jesus. He had kept the law scrupulously, it appeared—not only the minutae, but also the major commands of loving God and neighbor. He was a model young man, indeed, from the point of view of any set standards. But, according to the story, this did not satisfy the young man himself. He wanted still another specific command, but Jesus had one too great for him—that he sell all his possessions, give them away to the poor, and live the sort of life that he, Jesus, was living. Such sacrifice of social standing and security, such going out on one's naked own, was something utterly different from the requirements of Jewish law or of the gentlemanly code of his rich associates. Jesus was asking him to abandon both these and to live in the socially formless, self-directed way Jesus himself lived. To go in this way beyond the law was to step into what I call supralegalism, and for this the young man had no inclination.

Many supralegalists have appeared in history, but not enough. Jesus will serve as an excellent example, for he gave us the formula for the type in his famous statements that can be paraphrased: "You have heard other people, the legal teachers and fathers, even Moses himself, say to you that such and such are the rules and laws for your conduct under God; but I say that these are quite inadequate; the truth is that you should do thus and so."

Here is, indeed, an approach differing from that of legalism. The heart of legalism is that the individual delegates his responsibility for moral decision and takes a ready-made code, a blueprint, as his guide. He finds peace and satisfaction in doing the letter of the code. The heart of supralegalism, on the other hand, is that a man's own ideal world has become so vivid and self-sufficient that it subordinates both the id and the negative agents of his social urge alike, and he identifies himself with the ideal. Consequently, in leaving the demands of society to set up "superior" criteria, one becomes a law to oneself. Of course, this is only a partial experience. The supralegalist will still go about "decently" clothed and observe much the larger part of society's demands. Jesus had little patience with those who rebuked his disciples for munching grain heads as they crossed a field, but I cannot believe that he himself ate pork or did heavy work on the Sabbath. The demands of the codes of society are by no means totally flouted. But in the supralegalist a higher law with a greater power and dignity takes over on more important matters.

Such dual allegiance must be really of the individual's own creation for him to be called a supralegalist. One who is brought up in two worlds, taught them by his parents or church so that he feels that the ordinary code of the world is something always subject to correction from teachings of the church or of the "Christian way of life," has, as we saw, simply a divided legalistic allegiance. He has had both of these from society, and the sanctions of both are his social center. But, when Luther challenged the Church and the princes alike and asserted his freedom to follow the law of God as he had worked it out within himself and said, "Here I stand; I can do nothing else," he was a supralegalist.

Most supralegalists have left to their followers a code of laws which became a basis of legalism to them. Or codes have been drawn up in their names. So the early Communists had a sense of right that made them discard the old Russian codes; but, when they came into power, they allowed little freedom of judgment to their followers. Similarly, the Franciscan order made rules of discipline out of what Francis had said should be one's attitude toward the humble and poor. In some later Franciscans, the teaching survived in spontaneous life, and they, like Francis himself, lived creatively by self-prompted devotion to an ideal that was actually a part of their own psyches. But, as I said above, to live by the rule of an order, so long as the rule remains external to oneself or is observed as the rule of the order, is legalism. A Franciscan has always had to be more than a dutiful member of the order to be a true follower of Francis.

Ethical creativity, like creativity in music or the plastic arts, rises above all rules. The schools of music or painting correctly say that only those may break the traditional rules of form and harmony who know the rules. The schools themselves can teach only the rules and applaud when a pupil breaks into spontaneous creation. A school cannot teach spontaneous creation at all. Similarly in ethics; to reduce the conduct of Jesus, Gandhi, or Francis to rules is "imitation" which does not reproduce. It is to reduce their supralegalism to a new legalism.

One of the most extraordinary things about Jesus was that his teachings were not codes or rules at all. His followers have desperately tried to make some of his sayings into rules, as when some men take the saying about nonresistance literally and become conscientious objectors or when others take his remark about divorce literally and refuse to recognize divorce. To take some of Jesus' remarks as literal obligation and to explain away others seems to me a bit arbitrary. But Christians have almost universally done this. So the Catholic Church traditionally makes a law out of Jesus' prohibition of divorce, but it has rejected his teaching about castration and nonresistance. Origen insisted that Jesus would not have meant literally that a person hit on the right cheek should turn the other; for, he argued, Jesus would have been talking of ordinary circumstances, and actually if a right-handed man hits you, he hits you on the left cheek. The whole should be taken "figuratively" and was not a real law at all. This from a man who castrated himself because he took literally Jesus' saying that some have castrated themselves for the Kingdom of Heaven's sake!

To understand the teachings of Jesus, one cannot thus take as law what pleases oneself and explain the rest away; one must see his teaching as a whole, a unit, to be treated alike throughout. Apart from the problem of what Jesus actually taught, the teachings as they stand ascribed to him in the Gospels offer one of the few schools for supralegalism. It will pay to look at the teachings of the Sermon on the Mount, as presented in the fifth to the seventh chapters of Matthew, to illustrate this.

The Sermon begins with the utterly paradoxical Beatitudes, which end by blessing men who are persecuted and reviled by society, men who have a saltiness of their own that will savor society. That is, he calls for individualism. Beside this is put a completely contradictory picture, namely, that righteous men have a light which other men will find attractive. We should, accordingly, let our light shine so that man will be drawn to God by it. Will then, other men persecute us for our righteousness or give glory to God for it? Let the contradiction stand for a moment.

The text goes on at once to have Jesus say that he comes to fulfill the law, not to destroy even a single letter of a single word. What he proposes to do is to go not against, but quite beyond, the legalism of the Pharisees. How is this to be done? Jesus at once proceeds to destroy, not technicalities, but the foundations, of Jewish law. The first is truly a "going-beyond." The law against killing, he says, is fulfilled only when we give up anger, the smallest vituperation, or grudge-bearing and let anyone take what he wants from us rather than go to court. If this is what it means to obey the law against killing, then we are all murderers. The law, as

law, is made so all-inclusive that we can never get any satisfaction from it, for we disobey it constantly.

Similarly, a man who looks at a woman with an impulse
of desire, Jesus says, has thereby committed adultery with
her. Pull out your eyes if they fire you; cut off your hand if
you masturbate; and, as I have mentioned, Jesus said in another place: castrate yourself if necessary to control yourself. So we are all adulterers! The text goes on at once to
forbid divorce, which alone of all this passage or of all the
Sermon the Catholic Church takes literally. Of course, to a
man, who considered a stray look adultery, divorce and re-
marriage would also be adultery. Our question is: what is
Jesus doing throughout this sermon? Only in view of the
whole can we appraise a part. Clearly he is setting up no
legalistic code.

Oaths, said the good old law, shall be true and not per-
jured. Jesus says, never swear at all, simply say Yes or No,
for anything beyond this comes from evil. So far as I know,
only such sects as the Quakers take this teaching literally.
Then follows the breakdown of the old command of an eye
for an eye, the basic statement of justice in society: *one* eye
for *one* eye; not a destructive revenge, but fair damages and
compensation. Out the window with this, says Jesus. Let
any man strike or rob you without resisting him, and, as to
distinguishing between friend and enemy in your attitude,
that is all wrong. Love everyone alike as God does. And
soon he says the same thing again, that, unless we forgive
others as God forgives, we cannot be forgiven by God. It
could be argued that this pulls God's forgiveness down to
our level rather than raises ours to his, since a truly forgiving
God could forgive our lack of forgiveness. But that is
clearly not the intent of the passage. Jesus is teaching that
man should forgive all, as God is ready to forgive us all. The
Church, of course, and, if Jesus is correctly reported, even

Jesus himself never did accept God's universal forgiveness, since both taught that God's rage harries men eternally in hell-fire if they do not please him by repenting and believing.

With this, we get for the first time Jesus' point of reference. Man must not live by human standards in any sense, but by the standards and ways of God himself. How do we know those divine standards? Psychologically, Jesus is saying we should come into a higher life in the social context of God himself. Only there do we envisage the life of God in contrast to the standards given us by human society, even human society at its best. The whole Sermon centers in the one impossible command, that we be perfect as God himself is perfect. The new sort of legalism begins to appear, and it is indeed a supralegalism.

But the Sermon goes on relentlessly. How do we relate ourselves to this God, this Father in heaven? First, by avoiding all human acclaim for our virtue. We are to do our good deeds in secret, not let the left hand know what the right is doing. Jesus has in fact here reversed himself and told us to hide our light under a bushel, not to let others "see our good works" at all. No two commands could be more directly opposite, but the early Christians who compiled the Sermon thought that the two belonged together, as probably they belonged together in Jesus' own mind. The same rule applies to our prayer life, Jesus says, for it is to be utterly private and simple. Similarly with our fasting.

Then Jesus turns to the "practical" side of life, the money-and-property side, and sets up complete antipathy between God and Mammon. One cannot serve both, he says to us, as he said to the rich young man. Give no thought to the future; live by what comes each day, as do the daisies in the field. Lay up no treasure on earth; get nothing ahead. Take one day's trouble at a time. Obviously, no society can live in such a way. The Church tried to turn this into a counsel for the monks, but even they as groups could not live by it. They retired to monasteries which in general were ordered and financed. Modern Protestants have dismissed it as "interim ethic," to be practiced during the very few years before Jesus returned. Very clever; but I doubt it. India, without Jesus, has much more often put the ideal into practice than has the West, since reliance or chance receipts from begging has there for millennia been considered one of the basic requisites of true holiness. One of the ecclesiastical members of the Corporation of Yale years ago rebuked me sharply for saying that Jesus taught men improvidence. He was himself a rich man.

Enough has been said of the Sermon to show that it teaches supralegalism in contrast to legalism. Logically and practically, it presents us with a completely impossible picture. As Luther once said of the Sermon: "This word is too high and too hard that anyone should fulfill it." I can only infer that this was precisely its intent. Here is no blueprint of code or laws which man can keep, any more than man can do his good secretly while he lets the light of his righteousness shine for all to see. None of us can claim to deserve God's love or forgiveness on the ground that we love our enemies as dearly as we love our friends. We are all perjurers, adulterers, murderers. The Sermon has presented as travesties any such compromises with ideal conduct as appear in the basic laws of society and has told us that we must live by standards other than those of society's codes or we have no place in the kingdom of God. But it has not given us a new code.

Has Jesus given us a richer law than the lawyers of his day, the Pharisees? Yes, a higher Law, but not higher laws. As the Sermon stands, his very contradictions and hyperboles force us to supralegalistic independence of judgment.

The one thing that he has taught in all this is that the legalist approach, that of defining and limiting responsibility, falls far short of a free, spontaneous, creative approach to life's problems and to one's relations with God and man. There is no more point in quoting Jesus for strict or no divorce laws than in approving Origen's solution of his sex problems or than in refusing to take an oath in court or to defend our society from attack.

What does the Sermon teach, then? Only that a calculating aproach will never bring us to full ethical conduct and that each man must find God for himself and live directly by ideals of his own perception. We cannot compromise with the right, but must have within us such visions of the ideal that legal requirements have no relevance. Of course, society may crucify us for our attitudes, but that has little to do with it. We live by the right as we construct visions of it, not by the blueprints of human society. In doing so, we can never become smug, for we will always fall so far short of our ideal that our own feeling will be that of constant guilt. With such moral instruction as the Sermon gives us, we can never have any sense of right within ourselves, for, of course, we can never live by its teachings. Always to strive, always to feel we have failed—this is the heart of what Jesus is made to offer. When others praise us for our virtues, we can only say with sincerity (and with far more reason) what Jesus said: "Why do you call me good? No one is good but God." For the supralegalist, there is no relative good, no compromise. One may not agree with Jesus that any property is so wrong that we may not look ahead even as far as tomorrow; that our personal security is of no account whatever as compared to complete love for everyone, even if they are beating and robbing us; and in his blanket condemnation of sex, even to thinking that a stray look puts one into deepest sin. But Jesus is saying to all of us that our sense of right cannot be compromised, however much the world may wink at compromise, demand compromise, condemn us for not compromising. The world and its verdicts have little importance, says this teaching. You, stumbling along to fulfill your ideals, never succeeding, never satisfied, you and your ideals are the criterion, and you, if you are a supralegalist, must hate your failures, but never despair, only be made more determined by them.

Paul certainly had a great deal of this when he wrote: "If you are led by the Spirit, you are not under the law." He goes on, in the fifth chapter of Galatians, to give a list of the "works of the flesh"—that is, sins—a list which includes, not only the recognized ones, but "strife, jealousy, anger, self-ishness, carousing, and the like." In contrast, the Spirit leads one into "love, joy, peace, patience, kindness, goodness, faithfulness, gentleness, self-control; against such there is no law." Paul means that to live in this way is indeed no longer to live under laws, but beyond laws altogether, in supra-legalism. There is little satisfaction in such a life, except the satisfaction of compliance to a great compulsion. But some people can live in no other way, and they have been the salt of the earth.

The Church, of course, had to reject this. It kept some of it for the monks, but, insofar as they were living by the monastic "rule," as we have said, they too were legalists, not supralegalists. Supralegalism has never been an important part of organized Christianity. It could never play a large part in any organized religion.

This is the Jewish-Christian type of supralegalism, for the great prophets had similarly taught that the fulfillment of literal commands of sacrifice and the like had little value. What really counts, they said, is justice, love, kindness, hu-mility, and these the prophets left to the later rabbis to formulate into laws.

The Greeks or, rather, the Greek philosophers taught another approach to supralegalism. It has already been mentioned that the Greeks liked to think that their laws had been given by God or by a lawgiver inspired by divinity. But the Greek approach to law differed from those of both the Jews and the Romans. Where the Jewish instinct was to refine into more and more specific provisions the laws of the ancient code (mitigated always by a fair sense of justice) and the Romans had invented a legal system of predictable application and systematic approach, the Greeks paid relatively little attention to the elaboration of such ancient codes as appear in Hesiod or to organic development of their own legal principles. Like people of every civilization, the Greeks had very definite codes of conduct, especially in matters of religion and courtesy. But, when it came to civil and criminal law, they appealed to juries chosen from the citizens largely by lot, who were not experts in law at all. Any such thing as respect for precedent, the very essence of legal stability, could never be expected from such a popular mob. The appeal was always, therefore, that of the demagogue to the emotions, fears, hopes, greeds, and, at best, to the popular sense of fair play. Our best modern lawyers dislike jury trials because it is so difficult to keep a jury within the framework of predictable and orderly law. With a jury of five hundred, an outcome could never be predicted. Decorum, dignity, kindness up to a point, devotion to the state—these were what the Greeks largely lived on. They so disliked excess that they not only drank in moderation, but made moderation—"Nothing too much" —one of their basic principles, at least in theory.

Consequently, when Greeks speculated on ethics, their approach differed thoroughly from those of either Jewish tradition or of Jesus. The Greek idealists also saw vividly that to live by such law as society as a whole could sanction gave hope of only the most meager ethical achievement. The Jewish prophets and Jesus had put above the law an ideal person, God, who was just, merciful, in a way utterly beyond men, while insisting that men must imitate him, be perfect as he is perfect. Most men, even most ecclesiastical leaders, have shrugged their shoulders and returned to legalism as a much more feasible way to attain the satisfaction which religion, by its basic nature, craves.

The Greek thinkers, too, wanted to give the individual a sense of creative ethical responsibility, but they would have had no use for the paradoxes and hyperboles of Jesus' essentially irrational approach. So they worked out the equally great moral conception of the middle road, which I shall begin to describe by examples.

What is true bravery, the Greeks asked? It is conduct midway between cowardice and foolhardiness. The brave man knows what he is doing. He will dive in to help a drowning man, but not if he himself does not know how to swim, and he will stop long enough to take off his heavy clothing. But he will not dive in at all if the man is in an impossible current that would sweep both irresistibly and at once over a great waterfall. Firemen do all possible to help people in a burning house and often die in their attempts, but the chief must watch constantly, and, if the situation is indeed hopeless, the roof clearly about to fall, he will not allow his men to enter. Bravery is the middle road.

What is generosity? It is, said the Greeks, midway between stinginess and profligacy. The Greeks obviously did not agree that a man with property could no more get into heaven than a camel go through the eye of a needle. The Greeks, in this, thought like us, thought, so far as I can see, as a man must if a society such as ours is to exist. But penury, grasping for more and more, was for them as offensive as profligacy or financial irresponsibility. We must have property, but we cannot hang onto it when others need. The middle way lies between wasting one's substance, lending money to a crook, promoting visionary and hopeless schemes, on the one hand, and, on the other, being hard and insensible to the needs of men and society. Generosity is not an ideal of unlimited giving, but a middle way. Real generosity requires a great deal of intelligence, as the "philanthropoid" directors of our foundations are discovering.

Similarly, kindness lies between harshness and softness (and great is the parent who finds it); strength of character lies between weakness and stubbornness; sexual purity, between frigidity and whoremongering.

But how can we find this middle way? Only by rational analysis of oneself and the circumstances. Each man, with these principles in mind, must approach every situation ready to take responsibility for his own decisions. As soon as he falls back on a social custom, a teaching of the church, a precept of the rabbis, he has lost his supralegalism and returned to legalism. But the middle road is a difficult one because only the intelligent and heedful, and only those when not driven by neurotic compulsions, can walk it; and even they are aware that they are as often wrong as right. It is an invisible road, one to be kept, like a course in midocean, only when our sights are taken by the heavenly bodies or by compass and maps that tell us not what to do but show us the whole sea and make it possible for us to chart our own course.

Indeed, we have seen that the people of antiquity talked less and less about the middle road and looked increasingly to an orientation in the law of nature, the supreme law behind and above all particular laws. The law of nature was the right account, the true way not only for men but for the stars. In this universal right, men must indeed have universal references; the laws of cities, even of the Roman Empire, were quite secondary and local beside the one great law of the all. Men must submit to this as fate, and make their lives conform to it as right. When Philo discovered this law, his Jewish code became to him merely a handy approximation for ordinary people. He obeyed it to help such people keep to the only right they could ever know, the right of specific laws of conduct. But a completely other and greater world of right lay beyond this way of living, and anyone with true intelligence would learn to live by it.

Again that hard word, "intelligence." No wonder that the ancients themselves knew they were demanding the superhuman. How, in the name of common sense, was one to know anything as vague as this law beyond laws, know it clearly enough to live by it? Philo said that the mind of man could not remotely compass it. Only when the light of our own minds sets, he said, can the light of higher perception shine in. We have again begun to talk a language unintelligible to most men. Supralegalism is beyond most of us, whether in the paradoxes of Jesus, the rationalism of the middle road, or later antiquity's immediate perception of the law above laws. But its difficulty must not blind us to the fact that many of the greatest religious geniuses of all ages have found their religious experiences in it.

In terms of our psychological analysis, what is happening seems clear. The supralegalist has gone quite beyond the demands of the socially conditioned compulsions and found, or projected, a new society, a right, an ideal with which his ego so definitely identifies itself that the urges of the id and the pressure of society through his impulse to social conformity become relatively unimportant. As Paul said in Stoic terms, his "citizenship is in the universe."

We shall never agree as to whether the content of such an ideal is a matter of creation by the individual or, as it seems to him, is perception of a spiritual reality of which he is a part, but which is quite outside him at the same time. I suspect that the process is very similar to that which makes a creative scholar—the process of induction. The creative mind observes many phenomena and suddenly perceives that the data point to a new principle that no one who has handled them before had thought of. The creative scholar can never tell you how he reached his conclusion. What suggested it to him, if he can tell you, will be some quite trivial details, like the apple that is said to have fallen on Newton's head or the lamp in the Pisa Cathedral that suggested so much to Galileo. Often he is wrong, and his guess, his new perception, will have to be discarded. But often he is right, and science or mankind will have taken a new step toward understanding through his perception. The supralegalist is like this. Given the facts of human relationship, he sees implications in it that no one else can see.

So Wilson suddenly announced that the best outcome of World War I would be a peace without victory. This, of course, was before we got into the war ourselves, when he himself thoroughly abandoned such a solution. But perhaps he was right at first; the last war, if there ever be one, may well be a war in which neither side wins, so that both sides really give up all hope of solving man's problems by arms and seriously try another way. My point is not to argue the rightness or wrongness of Wilson's statement, but to say that I doubt that he himself could have told anyone how he came to such an amazingly original point of view, such a dream of right beyond all the "realism" of men.

Supralegalism, however, has its dangers and possible perversions. Obviously, supralegalism has led to perversion when the individual withdraws entirely from the recognized sanctions of society into schizophrenia. It is possible that all real supralegalists have a touch of schizophrenia, though on that I have no knowledge. Clearly, however, sheer madness is the logical end of disregarding too completely the rules and experience of society.

A still-more-dangerous perversion of supralegalism presents itself in men who get visions of a right beyond the accepted rights and turn out to be desperately dangerous and destructive. Hitler himself said in essence, like Jesus, that the ordinarily accepted codes of morality are quite inadequate, indeed utterly wrong. But he said that men would come to successful living only as they flouted the Jewish-Christian ideals of kindness and justice and learned to follow a man great enough to lie, cheat, make contracts and break them, as he led the strong people, the people made strong in the leader's strength, to the peace of victory and murderous supremacy. He appealed really not to an ideal at all, but to the id, with its passion for aggression and dominance. Clearly, it takes more than flouting old customs to make a supralegalist or to make one we can safely tolerate.

Perhaps, to account for the psychological adjustment of people of this type, we should have a religious category that we call "sublegalism." The "shadow" of legalism, if I may use Jung's term, is "pharisaism," where respect for the law becomes love of self for obeying the law. The code, which should lead us into the social orientation, has become in such a case a means of indulgence of the id in antisocial aggression. We refuse to "accept" people who do not live by our codes, people whom the rabbis called the *Am Haaretz* and our upper classes call "common" or "bounders." So do we strengthen our own self-righteousness. Similarly, the shadow of the supralegalist is the sublegalist. Many religious leaders who are convinced that they flout law and custom for their higher perceptions of right are like the thugs and gangsters who actually let the id go in full gratification and call doing so the higher right. Sailing through a technical flaw in the law to ruin a competitor or a partner can be called business acumen and take one to the forefront of society, as it has done many of our families of princely wealth. It, too, is sublegalism. But, clearly, I do not have such freedom from the law in mind in discussing supralegalism. Society is safe only insofar as the vast majority of us are reliable legalists. The id can present itself to our conscious minds in the guise of the ideal, representing itself as having a fresh perception of morality, and it can completely fool our conscious selves. When this happens to a teenager we recognize a delinquent, whereas the boy sees in himself a hero. It will appear throughout this book that I have a very high opinion of the value of the id. But, when it comes in the sheep's clothing of an ideal to make us violate basic social requirements, it can justify us in any crime, even in such vast criminality as the burning of millions of Jews.

I know no simple litmus paper by whose changing color we can recognize the validity of our motives. Man's safe road is the road of legalism, but all moral progress has come from supralegalists. Some men make their greatest contribution by daring to challenge the safe and sane. To allow departure from the code, however, is to open the gates to abuse and crime. Personally, I believe that society must take the risk of tolerating supralegalists and not crucify them. But the greatest risk in supralegalism is always taken by the individual, since society will not normally approve of his feeling that he knows a better and higher right than other men. Most of us will always be quite content to accept society's rules and let the id express itself as it may in covert vagaries. Only a few of us can or should settle the matter by going our own way.

Orthodoxy

Orthodoxy presents an approach to religion altogether different from the two we have been considering. Legalism and supralegalism seemed forms of religion conducted before a curtain whose design, whether traditional or painted by oneself, consisted mainly of rules of conduct. But the questions, "What shall I do to be saved?" or "safe," or "secure," or "at peace," can have another sort of answer, one which has to do primarily, not with our activity, but with our thought-world. The key word of the religion of legalism or conduct is "obey," of the other, "believe." The growing boy or girl early becomes concerned with questions of the meaning of life, and in popular parlance it is often the belief, not the acts, that are taken to mark an adult as being religious.

If a man says of himself or others say of him that he "does not believe in God," this supposedly marks him as being "irreligious." Now that the modern world has discovered so much about man and nature that it can no longer unite the whole into a compact credo, modern man often feels that he has lost the "meaning" of life. He must, as I pointed out in Chapter One, escape from this feeling into a clarity of knowledge. "Without a stable concept of the object of life, man would not consent to go on living and would rather destroy himself than remain on earth, though he had bread in abundance," said Father Zossima in *The Brothers Karamazov*. "The truth will set you free," we are taught. This has been said about so many conflicting "truths" that we must recognize that the "freedom" comes from a *sense* that we have the truth, rather than from the content of any given "truth." The traditional Protestant belief that the Bible is "true"; the neo-Protestant "freedom in Christ"; the Catholic belief that the Church has the truth, the peculiar truths of

Christian Science, Jehovah's Witnesses, and a hundred other forms of the Christian tradition—as well as humanism, Zen, Islam—all these give the same sense of clarity in understanding and hence peace with "freedom."

The freedom is actually release from the crushing chaos of the tremendum. "I believe; help thou mine unbelief." In the New Testament, the Fourth Gospel summarizes the message of Christianity in these terms: "He that believeth in me, though he were dead, yet shall he live." The history of the early Church presents us with a loyalty unto death, but also with that intense drive toward the "correct" formulations which produced the great creeds. In Christian worship, "I believe" rivals the sacraments themselves as the high point of the ritual. Like the jury that condemned Socrates, the ferocity with which the Church has treated heretics attests to the fundamental importance to Christians of "knowing the truth."

The great majority of men, we saw, take their patterns of conduct from their society or traditions, get them ready-made as blueprints; most people get their patterns of belief in the same way. How may we know that what we believe is really the truth? "Everybody says so"; or "the priest or church says so"; or "the creed says so"; or "our old men tell us"; or "the best people say so"; or, simply, "my mother or father used to believe"—these are only examples of the usually implicit footnotes to all men's beliefs on most subjects, to most men's beliefs on all subjects. This is by no means the attitude of simple and weak minds alone. Often the human mind fears itself, and we shrink from our own thinking.

A famous example of this was Cardinal Newman of the last century, one of the keenest minds of his age, who makes it all very clear in his *Apologia pro Vita Sua*. Newman left Anglicanism for the Roman Church because, as he summarizes it in the Preface, the Roman Church subdued his reason and conquered his heart. He wanted above all to feel that what he believed was right and true, and he well knew that his agile "reason" could find arguments for anything his "heart" desired, arguments which would convince others and, worst of all, convince himself. I cannot say how it came about that a sense of ignorance on any point aroused in him such insecurity. Perhaps this was his characteristic by birth; perhaps his attitude could be traced to childhood experiences and conditioning. His brother tells something of his youth and makes it clear that, though his mind had extraordinary powers to see the force of arguments, he did not trust it. At fourteen, he was reading Tom Paine and David Hume, much impressed by their reasonableness. "He found pleasure in thinking of the objections" to orthodoxy. He once said that to the age of fifteen he lived a life of sin, with a very dark conscience and a very profane spirit. The sin of this pious, observant, and precociously studious young man would seem to have been that he was relying on the fascination of his own critical powers. Indeed, he says just this in the *Apologia* when he again describes that religious awakening:

> I was brought up from a child to take great delight in reading the Bible; but I had no formed religious convictions until I was fifteen. Of course I had a perfect knowledge of my Catechism. . . . When I was fifteen a great change of thought took place in me. I fell under the influences of a definite creed, and received into my intellect impressions of dogma, which, through God's mercy, have never been effaced and obscured.[2]

Protestantism, he came later to see, had shown all too clearly that to approach the Bible with an undirected mind could lead to indefinitely diversified and unpredictable conclusions. "Every creed has texts in its favor," he wrote, "and

[2] John Henry Newman, *Apologia pro Vita Sua* (New York: 1900), pp. 1–4.

again texts which run counter to it; and this is generally confessed." [3] When a man with a dogma already settled reads the Bible, he has great comfort in piecing biblical statements together that seem to represent that dogma, he explained.[4] But the pieces themselves could reflect human perversity quite as well as divine truth if put together without authoritative guidance. When he was established at Oxford, he attacked the orthodoxy of the Regius Professor of Divinity because, as Newman said, he "maintained that Religion is distinct from Theological Opinion, that it is but a common prejudice to identify theological propositions methodically deduced and stated, with the simple religion of Christ . . . that speculation always left an opening for improvement." [5]

All this was impossible for Newman. Indeed, Newman's great search that finally led him to Rome was for a body of teaching completely and ultimately certified, so that his mind could stop at last the uncertainty of arguments and reasons and rest on an undisputed authority. Over against the certainty of Catholicism (ultimately the Catholicism guaranteed by papal decree and organization), he saw only atheism (as another dogmatism), and the choice between them, he repeatedly stated, was absolute; no middle ground existed.[6] Something within him, clearly, was tearing out the middle ground, giving him a sickening vertiginous attraction toward atheism. Obviously, this something within him was his own reason, and, since atheism presented chaos and utter tragedy to his emotions, he must give up his reason and accept an objectively certified body of doctrine. The tensions within him were so great that something radical had

[3] *Ibid.*, p. 87.
[4] *Ibid.*, p. 9.
[5] *Ibid.*, p. 57.
[6] *Ibid.*, p. 198.

to go. His craving for the security of certainty balanced his drive to critical analysis before which—in such honesty and power as it asserted itself in Newman—all certainty dissolves. Which should he kill within himself? He finally chose to kill his reason, as he called it, which meant not his power of ratiocination, but his critical questioning of anything fundamental. He gave up his inductive mind, his power of forming conclusions from data, to enjoy the peace of making deductions from what his faith accepted as the self-evident axioms of the Church.

> From the time that I became a Catholic, of course I have no further history of my religious opinions to narrate. In saying this I do not mean to say that my mind has been idle, or that I have given up thinking on theological subjects; but that I have had no variations to record, and have had no anxiety of heart whatever. I have been in perfect peace and contentment; I never have had one doubt.[7]

This happened when he came to believe "that the Catholic Roman Church was the oracle of God." [8] All beliefs now became corollary to this one. He still could not logically and reasonably explain his belief, which was a matter, as the church said, of faith. But "ten thousand difficulties do not make one doubt." [9] He had at last come into that "certitude" which alone could give him peace.[10]

Millions of highly intelligent contemporaries of ours, few with the honest awareness of Newman, have done much as he did as they find peace without criticism. Many sorts of orthodoxies now quiet our critical uneasiness. I am writing, not of orthodox Christians of any one sort, or Moslems, or Jews, or Christian Scientists, or Zen Buddhists, but of ortho-

[7] *Ibid.,* p. 238.
[8] *Ibid.,* p. 239.
[9] *Loc. cit.*
[10] *Ibid.,* pp. 19-21, 214-216, 238.

doxy as a religious—that is, psychological—phenomenon, which as such changes little from one group to another.

The orthodoxy of a Marxist certifies very different ideas from those of a Catholic or a follower of Hitler, but, *qua* orthodox, followers of any of these groups all hate the liberals, what is in Newman's terminology the middle ground between atheistic and Catholic certainty. A person of this temper can admire a strong enemy who "knows what he wants," as an orthodox capitalist can admire a "Red" personally, though he fears and attacks him. Both agree in despising the liberal who, seeing merit on both sides, seems really groping in the dark, lacks "certitude." The rebellion of most people rests, not on personal thought, but on their accepting a new orthodoxy; we have all been bored when such converts have given us the "party line." There is orthodox literary criticism, literary style, economic theory, Freudianism, stimulus–response psychology, and many, many others. The common denominator among the orthodox of all kinds is not what they believe, but that they have accepted a pattern of thought as true. Their blueprints have come to them ready-made, and their "hearts faint not" in an accepted account of the nature of things, to the point that, if they really carry through, like Newman, "ten thousand difficulties do not make a doubt." Scholarly orthodoxy is often as impervious to argument or evidence as any other kind of orthodoxy.

That the doubts are really hidden in the unconscious appears in the murderous savagery with which the orthodox usually face heresy. Many profiteers have, of course, fattened themselves on the confiscated estates and ruined businesses of those they persecute, and many have used witch trials to avenge personal grudges, but some of the cruelest things have been done without a trace of such motives, simply from a frightened desire to destroy those who challenge one's faith. Where conviction begins, tolerance must end—at least tolerance within the circle of believers. Most of us can tolerate Communism in Russia, but even the most liberal of us would give short shrift to genuine Communist plotting to overthrow the state in America, and we are armed to the teeth to prevent the forcing of Communism on any now-"free," that is, capitalistic, country. Now I know nothing that proves ours to be the true philosophy of life; it is possible that the Russian faith in their "way" rests on a scheme of reality, human and social, which in the long run would develop man more than "the American way."

Only by faith can I believe, as I do, in the American way to the point that, if all else fails, I would have us fight to defend it. But this is faith on my part, faith in the orthodox tradition of my civilization, about what makes life meaningful. I do believe in the "propositions," as Lincoln called them, to which our society is dedicated, and I do not believe in those of Russia or China or, for that matter, of Spain or Saudi Arabia. I see in this no excuse for McCarthy's terroristic attempts to stifle all discussion and willingness to learn from other experiments. But that is because in this I have not the fully orthodox point of view. I doubt very much that even the United States has the whole truth. This I must admit as a Liberal who dislikes the orthodoxies of extremists, both left and right.

Orthodoxy lies so deep in the structure of human nature that, for all the terrors of reaction when orthodoxy goes too far, we actually cannot live without beliefs in the basic meaning of man's life. Does the state exist for the individual, or the individual for the state? Do we live in an orderly universe, one which in some way and to some extent the human mind can understand? Science is impossible without a belief in the latter, and government and society would "perish from the earth" without a firm answer to the former. My point, however, is that we now know enough about man to recognize that all the "propositions" are projections of dream patterns upon the basically unknown. That the projections about Christianity were made fundamentally by the first ecstatic Christians who thought that they had seen Jesus risen from the dead makes them projections none the less. And their being so makes them no less valuable as a basis for security if accepted by faith.

Actually, we all must live largely by orthodoxy. We may not accept orthodox Christianity or Judaism, but we could not carry through a day without a "stable concept of the object of life," at least as a working proposition. We may be too busy with physics or banking to recognize that our activity is carried on in a world of assumed values and objects. Our orthodoxy may function quite below the level of consciousness. But we would all perish if we lost altogether the security of a settled scheme of things, and this, for the most part, we inherit ready-made. Some people center their concept and experience of religion on it; it is part of the total religion of all men, whether we call it so or not.

Supraorthodoxy

There are a few, however, who basically question the validity and relevance of traditional schemes and systems and go on to what I call "supraorthodoxy." As in orthodoxy, one is concerned not with details but with over-all patterns of the meaning and destiny of man, with the nature of the universe and reality, and with the ultimate causation, so in supraorthodoxy we shall see men who crave total metaphysical patterns, but who cannot accept patterns given by tradition and must make new patterns for themselves.

The glory of the Hebrew tradition was its long line of supralegalists, a line which by no means ended with Jesus, even though it finally crystallized, for most Jews, in the elaborate legal formulations of rabbinic Judaism. In contrast, Greece in its prime produced a series of supraorthodox philosophers who, from Thales through Plato, Aristotle, Epicurus, and on to Plotinus, created one after another new cosmological and metaphysical frameworks, each original and individually perceptive. The Buddha also had a supraorthodox urge, whereas Jesus and Francis of Assisi had supralegalist ones. So large a number, however, of the greatest religious leaders—such as Paul, Origen, Aquinas, and Luther in Christianity alone—have had the urge to create a new metaphysical world for man that the type, if rare, deserves a special discussion. It has been one of the most important religious patterns in human experience.

Supraorthodox religion usually begins with an emotional experience, but quickly comes to express itself as an idea. Most of the supraorthodox go no further than to reorganize an orthodoxy in which they have been brought up. Augustine and Aquinas made creative reorganizations which many traditionalists gladly accepted as the true meaning of their orthodoxy. The idealism of Socrates-Plato (both had primary creative vision), on the other hand, left Greek traditional thinking completely and made a new world of questions, forms, and realities. Aristotle, a student of Plato, created a world almost as novel. Descartes and Hegel similarly seemed to spring forth *ex nihilo*, and Spinoza's pantheism had certainly little root in anything in his environment. Similar motives and psychological needs produce similar patterns of thought, but no creative thinker ever found full satisfaction in any other person's system— wherein appears the first element in the type we are now trying to understand. The supraorthodox has instinctively (if I may use this word in its popular sense) a negative reaction to the formulations of others. He may and will use bits, aspects, of other people's ideas, but he can feel satisfaction in them only as they seem to fit into a pattern essentially his own.

His satisfaction lies, not so much in the adequacy of his idea or phrase to express reality, as in the fact that, however poor a thing, it is his own. Indeed, my supraorthodox friends would rather be proved wrong than trite. To show the common element which marks a single type amidst all the individual differences, I shall discuss briefly two of the supraorthodox giants who were as unlike each other as possible.

The first, Benedict de Spinoza, was a relatively pure rationalist, at least in his form of presentation. His grandfather had fled to Holland among the first of the Portuguese Jews, like the first Pilgrims, to seek in the country of new freedoms a place where the Jews could again live in the way of their ancestors. In Amsterdam—the "New Jerusalem," as the Jews of the day called it—reaction tended to set in. Too often men recently escaped from persecution have themselves become persecutors. The Jews of the new community had had for generations to cover their own loyalties with a semblance of Catholic conformity, and many of those who went to Amsterdam kept what seemed valuable to them in Christian usages and beliefs. The leaders of the group believed that this had to be rigorously extirpated. Spinoza was by no means the only one expelled from the synagogue and Jewish fellowship for unorthodoxy. He himself offended, not by trying to reform conservative Judaism, however, but by going completely beyond its range.

From a foundation in rabbinic writings, in Maimonides, and probably in the *Zohar* of philosophic cabalism, he went on to Giordano Bruno and Descartes. Both the latter taught him to orient his metaphysics to the new science, and it was reported that Descartes specifically taught him that nothing ought to be admitted as true but what had been proved by good and solid reasons. The philosophy of Descartes had just been condemned by religious people of many sorts, so that for the Jews—themselves a tolerated group in Holland —to have sheltered a thinker with such ideas would not only have violated their own sensitivities, but would have invited reprisals. Spinoza was accordingly expelled from the synagogue and from all relations with Jews and was presumably banished from Amsterdam. He lived most of the rest of his life at The Hague as a grinder of beautifully made lenses. He said on learning of his expulsion: "This compels me to nothing which I should not otherwise have done." [11]

That really creative work of Spinoza, however, came from the stimulus of his disagreement with Descartes. His rejection of orthodoxy, whether Jewish or Christian, was so basic as to leave no problems. This came out in a letter to a Catholic who taunted him with his philosophic self-reliance and contrasted it with the certitude of ecclesiastical tradition. Spinoza asked him how he knew that Catholic Christianity was the best of religions when he knew nothing of the religions of India and elsewhere.

One of his commentators says the Spinoza's religion was essentially a free "cooperation with the order of the world as manifested in the nature of man and of society." [12] The same scholar repeatedly describes Spinoza's passionate love of God, an aspect of life that few would exclude from religion. Spinoza thought, however, that the way to this love of God led, not from the emotions, but from the understanding. In his early life, he called the love of God one of the few exceptions to the rule that no passions have any place in the life of a philosopher. But even in the early writings he says that the love of God arises from knowledge of God, which knowledge is the source of all knowledge. We

[11] F. Pollock, *Spinoza* (New York: 1899), p. 19.
[12] *Ibid.*, pp. 66 f.

may know God, he said, better than we know ourselves. As he grew older, all reference to passion in the love of God disappeared, and that love became indistinguishable from speculative knowledge. Man comes into happiness and true freedom only as he knows the "most perfect being" and so discovers his own part in the universal order and unity.

Spinoza accordingly began with theology—the study of the nature and being of God. With this established, he could, like Euclid, go on to what seemed to him the inevitable conclusion as to man's nature and duties. To orient his thinking to the best science of the day, he wrote as his masterpiece a book in one of the strangest forms in history. His *Ethics* is not connected discourse at all, but a series of books like Euclid's, each made up of theorems demonstrated by reference to Spinoza's initial assumptions. The satisfaction of thus expanding the implications of his major premises came from and contributed to the sense of expanding certitude. "Whoever has a true idea," he wrote in the *Ethics*,[13] "knows at the same time that he has a true idea, and cannot doubt the truth of the thing perceived. . . . No one who has a true idea is unaware that a true idea involves the utmost degree of certitude. . . . What can be found more clear and certain than a true idea, which may be the test for truth?" Such ideas, he assures us, are "produced by the pure operation of the mind." [14]

Psychologically, we have here the key to Spinoza's life. Like everyone else, Spinoza wanted the security of certitude. He theoretically identified religion with the fruit of such knowledge in a life of social justice, and in practice Spinoza, fading away with consumption while he continued his devoted thinking and writing, showed the most remarkable genius for justice and kindness. But he founded no

13 Part II, Proposition 43.
14 Pollock, *op. cit.*, p. 136.

school and refused ever to give up his cloistered life. He left his *Ethics* unfinished, and it was published posthumously. In fact, the meager details we have of his life suggest a person to whom expulsion and retirement brought relief, the relief he could find in concentrating on his own "certain" ideas and their logical implications.

His life centered in the true idea no less than Newman's; but, the more he came to the truth through criticizing the ideas of others and creating new ones for himself, the more certitude they brought him. Few will be able to take Spinoza's creative intellectual path to reality and security, but many of our greatest minds have been deeply inspired by him and probably will be for centuries to come.

Sören Kierkegaard I put alongside Spinoza because, beneath their obvious dissimilarities, they both show the supraorthodox pattern. Kierkegaard much more apparently than Spinoza was creating a metaphysical world out of his personal needs, but each found peace and security by creating his own.

Kierkegaard's chief personal problem was with his father, who almost absorbed his younger life, and yet for years Kierkegaard could not finish reading for his degree out of guilt-ridden revolt against his father. The son to a larger extent tried to relive, indeed had to relive, the father's deepest problems. The father had been a country lad, a shepherd boy who, in the loneliness of his physical and intellectual deprivations, cursed God at the age of twelve. A lifetime of repentance never removed from the father the feeling that this act had made him irredeemably accursed, so that the whole undercurrent of his life flowed thick with the murky silt of despair. When he became a man, though quite untrained, the father went to Copenhagen, made a fortune, and read the most abstruse works of theology and philosophy. He developed an amazing power in logical and metaphysical disputation, and the son recalled his breathless fascination as he listened to the father dominate any discussion in such fields. The father regarded the son as his peculiar vehicle of continuity and managed to transmit to the son his power for abstract thinking, along with the pathological sense of guilt with its need for an atoning self-torture that never atoned.

The result could not in the least resemble the untroubled sea of Spinoza's reasoning. The ordinary concerns of men gave no consolation to Kierkegaard. Even in his own great love affair he showed himself quite unable to find the ideal in the real, and in a way I have heard called "caddish" he finally broke off his engagement.[15] The essential cause of Kierkegaard's shrinking before the reality of Regina I shall not attempt to guess, but not far from the center must be his statement: "Without sin, no sexuality; without sexuality, no history." Regina was more fortunate than she then supposed. Kierkegaard could talk about life, love, and the ideal in a way that has moved many to find deeper meaning for their own life experiences; but his own life seems to have had little to offer except a compulsion that was far from caddish—the compulsion to construct the noblest thoughts he could.

In doing this, he had to break from his father while only more deeply following the father's pattern; he had to break from Regina to find more exalted spiritual love; he had to break from the Church to discover what seemed to him the heart of Christianity. "I am a man who must discover Christianity by himself, dig down to make it emerge from the perverted state it has sunk to." [16] Often he said with deep sincerity that he would not call himself a Christian at all; to know true Christianity was to know one's limitations. For

[15] Kierkegaard himself called it the act of a "cad, perhaps an arch-cad; . . . but at the same time it was exquisite chivalry." P. P. Rohde, *The Diary of Sören Kierkegaard* (London: 1961), p. 41.
[16] *Ibid.*, p. 148.

him, thinking had two dimensions—originality or perception and exemplification of one's ideas in daily life. So he wrote:

> There has probably existed many an author more acute and with greater genius than I, but I should like to see one who with keener acumen has reduplicated his very thinking to the second power of dialectics. It is one thing to be a keen thinker in books, another to reduplicate one's thinking in his own existence. . . . A thinker who fails to reduplicate the dialectics of his thinking never receives the final test of action. Only the ethical thinker, by acting, can safeguard himself against communicating illusions.[17]

His resolution of the guilt that haunted him was to create a God supernally good; then to fall in love with the God he had created; and then, like Paul, to lose his identity in that loving Father. What emerged, however, was his new supra-orthodox creation: "In my conception, to be victorious does not mean that *I* triumph, but the idea triumphs through me, even though it entails my being sacrificed." [18]

His most emphatic assertion was to deny any value in humanity, since all value is in God. He sought certitude as the basis of security, as did Spinoza and all others of the supra-orthodox. But Kierkegaard's certitude came from a faith which required the rejection of all orthodoxy, of the reason as master guide, for an apprehension, an assimilation of the truth revealed in faith to the whole man. He actually seems never to have questioned any important statement in the creeds, except that the organized church is an integral part of Christianity. Yet creedal statements of the truth meant nothing to him as objects of faith. True faith, from which alone he could hope for certainty, was a gift of grace, a direct action, not on the mind, but on the whole man. True

[17] *Ibid.*, pp. 111 f.
[18] *Ibid.*, p. 124.

faith leads man to action, Kierkegaard believed, and action arises from passion and the will.

Instead of creating a new series of abstract propositions about truth, Kierkegaard the existentialist bade man to move out beyond orthodoxy to apprehend himself—in mind, passions, and will, as subordinated totally to the will of God. Kierkegaard's originality consisted primarily, I believe, in his refusal to make a system of rationalistic propositions as all before him had tended to do. He did so on the ground that systems could be made only from lifeless abstractions.

Yet most of my readers will feel that Kierkegaard really made a system out of denying what seemed to him to characterize other people's systems and that he was getting his certitude and security from a rationalization of life's very paradoxical character and from its resolution in what seemed to him a direct action of God's grace. His faith was faith in his own perceptions, if not in his power to systematize them. He made a great virtue of his suffering, and in doing so felt that he stood alone among men. His father's guilt became his own guilt and the guilt of the human race. As Spinoza walked the true classicist road of form which dominated his period, Kierkegaard romanticized in the age of romanticism. Werther himself seems to be speaking when Kierkegaard says:

> Of all torments, being a Christian is the most terrible; it is —and that is how it should be—to know hell in this life. . . . We shudder to read about the sufferings a beast undergoes when it is used for vivisection; yet this gives only a glimmering of the pain involved in being a Christian: to be kept alive in a state of death.[19]

His writings now have their chief appeal to people divided among guilt, fear, and idealism, as was Kierkegaard himself.

[19] *Ibid.*, pp. 200 f.

TYPES OF RELIGIOUS EXPERIENCE

That is, supraorthodoxy characterizes those who, on any ground or in any way, have refused to take the current explanations of life as a basis for their adjustment and who must create a sort of intellectual adjustment for themselves, one which may or may not be truly rational. The faithful followers of Kierkegaard are now so numerous and, in Protestant circles, so powerful that they represent an orthodoxy against which Kierkegaard might well have turned with distaste, as he turned against the idealism of his own day. This we cannot say, for his undisciplined spirit might have been tamed by the Orphic music of his own creative words reverently echoed. He died prophetically expecting such a reception of his teachings, but he never lived to see himself have any appreciable following.

Both Kierkegaard and Spinoza got their security from their originality, which began with their break with tradition. What I call supraorthodoxy is religious security that arises in this way from one's own intellectual creativity in metaphysics or theology. Obviously, if such a form of religious experience is unusual, it is among the most important forms in human history, especially in the West.

Aestheticism

Religion has appeared largely to be the search for form in what we usually experience as the formless and unpredictable world outside and within us. Accordingly, it need cause no surprise when that whole approach to form which we call "aestheticism" appears to be a type of religious experience in its own right. For the Greeks, athletic form; in many places throughout the world, the dance; architectural forms, painting, sculpture, music, and literary formulation in poetry and prose—all these have provided "sacred" forms and have been utilized by organized or traditional religions everywhere, primarily because they can give the satisfaction demanded for religious experience. The craving for security through form rises chiefly from unconscious levels and is gratified as we find form in any way. To create form or to share in the created forms of others gives a real experience of form within oneself and hence a real religious experience.

Like other types of religion which we have been describing, aestheticism falls into two categories—that of the creator and that of one who shares the creation of others, as appears in the contrast between the experience of a man in reading Milton and that of Milton himself in writing or between a skilled orator and his audience. Indeed, in some arts a third category arises, as when an actor interprets *Hamlet* to an audience or a pianist renders a composition of Hindemith. We need not go here into the question disputed among musicians, whether a performer can himself be creative, for even the stubbornest admit that, although an organist playing Bach is not creative in the sense that Bach was, in playing he is far more creative than is the audience. One reading poetry for himself has the poet's creativity at second hand, and I need make the point no sharper than to say that the religious value of the aesthetic experience at second hand is much less intense than that of the poet (or painter or sculptor) himself. A man is certainly impoverished if he cannot, through at least one form of art, forget the confusion of life in a sense of order.

Men have so long contrasted the athlete with the aesthete that it may surprise some of my readers to see them put together. Perhaps the athlete is tone-deaf, physically and emotionally, to the values of music; often the artist is himself color-blind to the perfection of form in a hurdle race, the golfer's drive, the skier's jump, the swing of the paddles in a racing eight, or the like. Very well. In talking about these experiences to Yale undergraduates, however, I have many times had a boy come up at this point to say that, for the first time, he really understood what I meant by the craving for form and the peace of mind that comes by finding it. One boy had found it in throwing the javelin; another, in the exquisite coordination of basketball. Those who care for young children know the importance of physical skills in the development of a child's psychic stability, not only as an outlet for competition and aggression, but through the act of formal precision in itself. And we who cannot ourselves perform on the trapeze really identify with those who do; it is we who fly to the waiting hands of our swinging partner. The delight of a crowd at an extraordinarily skillful catch and throw in baseball is aesthetic delight, expressed more noisily, perhaps, than our response to a beautiful poem or painting, but most deeply a delight in form. And still, like the Greeks of old, millions regard such great athletes as Babe Ruth with genuine reverence for the demigod. The Greeks put the crown of laurel on the heads of such people and stopped everything, even their wars, to watch them. The place given sports by the church schools of England and America basically recognizes the religious importance of physical form.

All this holds true, of course, for the dance. From the universal religious dances of savages to the exquisite Bacchanalia on Greek vases and to the spontaneous dancing in the aisles of the less conventional Protestant sects, the dance has been one of the most common religious rites. The religious procession is a form of dance, and it loses all value if sloppily done. The term "devotees of the ballet" is entirely proper, for the dance can arouse very real devotion in both dancers and observers in proportion to its formal perfection.

If religion be the quest for beauty, as it in large part is from the aesthetic point of view, beauty in the sense of perfection of form in shape and in motion, then we can hardly omit mentioning one of the most universal of religious acts—sexual intercourse. My anthropologist colleague, G. P. Murdock, has told me that the word for "beauty" in most languages has sexual connotations, so that apparently the perception of beauty in a mate, the achievement of a beautiful sexual relation, first taught man to distinguish between the beautiful and the ugly in a way which he has finally applied to all the other fields. The experience has provided one of the chief symbols of diety in India, and sexual relations as ritualistic acts of worship appear in an extraordinary number of civilizations of past and present. The effect of ritualistic intercourse on the devotee is by no means conveyed when we continue to sneer at it with the Old Testament prophets, and speak of the practice as "temple prostitution."

Christianity is fully aware of the importance of sex and marriage in religion and insists that marriage be "holy," a sacrament, from which no ecclesiastical tradition has been able to remove the universal interpretation that it should be creatively satisfactory to both parties in sexual relations. In nothing does prejudice more control judgment. Between the extreme attitude of the unconventional, that a beautiful sex act carries and conveys its own benediction, to the other extreme, which regards the act as degrading under any circumstances and sees abstention from it, "chastity," as the prime basis for the highest religious experience, there are a thousand local stations where most of us stop. It would be extremely interesting to treat sex as a type of religion in itself. But this would go beyond what could be presented to the general public.

The simultaneous reconciliation of the urges to dominate and to be dominated, to come into a higher life through the fusion of personalities, especially with one we regard as a beautiful personality and who responds to us beautifully—

these are not only the experiences of religion at its highest, but are both represented and achieved in beautiful intercourse as in nothing else man does. The craving that the child be identical with the parent is stated over and over in the myths of the East and culminated in the Christian Son, who was one with the Father. This craving finds its satisfaction in a relation with a person of the other sex, where we vacillate beautifully between being the child and the parent of our mate. What of this belongs here is that, when the vacillation of roles in a man–woman relationship properly synchronizes, man has found nothing in life more beautiful and nothing that more often recurs as a religious figure. Here man can find one realization of his religious longings for form—and hence a genuine religious pattern.

We have mentioned sex as only one aspect of the religion of aestheticism, for, whatever else may be required of sex to make it a religious experience, certainly without a sense of beauty it only repels, if it does not horrify.

The exercises of bodily movement are considered so remote from religion as we ordinarily use the term that it will seem more comfortable to most of my readers to consider the religious values of aestheticism in terms of aesthetic expressions commonly recognized as such—literature and "the arts." All branches of Christianity as well as most other religions use these constantly in attaining religious goals. Quakers have successfully kept visual beauty out of their forms and places of worship, but the Puritans could not do so; the meetinghouses in their villages have made New England a place of pilgrimage. One wonders whether the Bible would have achieved its great place in English and German life had the truly magical prose of the King James and Lutheran versions not so genuinely transposed, in places transcended, even the exquisite artistry of the originals.

Poets and musicians, whose works stimulate the religious

experience of others, have often found adequate religious experience for themselves in their own creations. Poets have said this over and again about themselves and their writing. Wordsworth and Coleridge combined in their *Lyrical Ballads* to show the universal in the commonplace or, as they phrased it, the supernatural in the natural and the naturalness of the supernatural. In "The Elements of Poetry," Santayana insisted directly on the ultimate identity of poetry and religion. Poetry, he says, takes the stray notes or symbols and, in putting them together into harmonies, leads us to comprehend the real. He himself saw the Catholic Church as a poem, "poetry become the guide of life"; it protected man from the unformed, which can be apprehended directly only in mysticism. To Santayana, the issue became basically what I am saying in this book—the problem of escaping the formless. Santayana saw the most effective way of doing this in poetic formulation, and so poetry was to him the highest type of religion, as religion in its highest form was poetry.

In his "Defense of Poetry," Shelley had eloquently said much the same, that one escapes from the flow of accidental impressions and gets "a habit of order and harmony" by recourse to the "poetical power." Shelley, like our modern Jeremiahs, believed that the sciences had engulfed man: "Man, having enslaved the elements, remains himself the slave." He, too, would abandon all study of phenomena and substitute religion for it. He did not urge us to go back to the creeds; we should find the true religion in poetry.

With deeper insight than either Shelley or Santayana, Arthur Davison Ficke, the American poet of the first two decades of this century, wrote:

> Probably all my poetry is nothing more nor less than the attempt to integrate my own personality—to crystallize all my random impulses and vague intuitions into something

tangible, clear, and reasonable. It is the effort to take all these loose-strewn materials, which exist in the mind of an idiot, and construct out of them a more or less orderly edifice. It is the undertaking to evolve a controlled intelligence out of an emotional chaos:—to provide clear, straight channels through which the murky streams of primordial feeling may flow.

One great advantage of this work of integration is that the integrated emotions take on an objective existence; and their nature can then be more easily observed and criticized than if they had remained unexpressed.

I doubt very much that this last was what most deeply drove Ficke to write his poetry. That he worked over his poems with assiduous care to try to bring them closer to a perfection he himself well knew he had not reached, that he "criticized" them—yes, certainly. But he did not write in order to criticize; he was writing, he said, in order to "integrate his own personality." As through poetry he "crysallized his random impulses," he changed the loose-strewn materials of his "idiot" mind into an orderly edifice —and clearly the orderly edifice he strove to create was even more himself than were the poems. A poem was a means to his end—the integration of himself. In the creation of his poems, Arthur Ficke found his new birth; his new spiritual, clarified existence; his true beauty. Like Paul, he "counted not himself to have attained" and so, by constant criticism, "pressed on to the mark of this high calling." Any distinction between Ficke and his poetry becomes artificial. It was his spiritual exercise as truly as prayer or the sacraments are to Christians. The phrase is exactly that of La Fontaine, "De la poèsie comme exercice spirituel."

As often happens in such a case, Ficke detested the forms of worship and belief of traditional religions in a way to recall Jewish and Christian scorn of the false gods of paganism. In this, he thought he was rejecting "religion." He could reject other religions because, seeker that he was, he found them indeed pagan in comparison to the true religion of making form in poetry.

We need not rehearse the remarks or study the ways of musicians to demonstrate that their art often takes the same place in their lives. Music has been defined to me as "ordered sound," and it is through this order that musicians have their experience. As Browning had Abt Vogler say:

> The rest may reason and welcome,
> 'Tis we musicians know.

Bach exemplified the matter most poignantly. He fully accepted the Church's teachings, but spent his life largely in vitalizing them through his music. Three days before he died, I have been told, he had a stroke which immobilized him; he kept his mind and power of speech, though he was blind and otherwise totally paralyzed. Under these conditions, he dictated to one of his sons *Aus tiefer Not* (Luther's German version of *De Profundis*), one of the most beautiful and original choral preludes he ever wrote. The words were those of theology, but the musical form which he created for the words gave him his real consolation in his ultimate *Not*. Had he wanted merely the theology, he could have recited the prayers and Psalms as words. This, precisely, did not suffice. Throughout his life, the words had taken on meaning as he could set them into the counterpoint of his own creativity.

Those are poor indeed who have not found the confusion of their lives at least temporarily resolved into form, that is, beauty, as they have listened to the creations of their companions. Orpheus with his lyre still has the divine power of stilling the savage beasts within us. Those who best know all forms of art will understand my identifying the expression of art, at first or second hand, with religious experience. The experience so warms and beautifies that I wish that I had a less frigid term for it than "the religion of aestheticism."

Symbolism and Sacramentalism

Two approaches to religion, symbol and sacrament, may be discussed together because both find their goals through an object or act in the material world itself, though not by the path of aestheticism. "An outward and visible sign of an inward and invisible grace," the official definition of a Christian sacrament, applies in fact to much more than the official seven sacraments of the Church. The crucifix, or crossing oneself, holy medals, a rosary (still better if blessed on the Holy Sepulchre or by the pope), the Stations of the Cross and their ritual—all and many more have importance far beyond the merely visible sign. We need not go into the distinctions now made between these and the official seven "sacraments," that is, between what the Church calls sacraments founded by Christ and "sacramentals" established by the Church. The Church insists that to be blessed by the pope is not a sacrament in the full sense, *ex opere operato*, but a person not brought up in the Church finds this distinction difficult to understand when he reads the extraordinary potencies officially ascribed to a rosary blessed at the Holy Sepulchre.

Again we are helped by our psychological rather than theological approach, for, psychologically, any rite or object which has the power of conveying religious benefit is, in our broad sense, a sacrament or a sacramental. When Professor T. R. V. Murti of Benares put a wreath of flowers around my neck, carried the cup of wine and bit of cake into the shrine of Shiva, and brought it out blessed and holy to give it to me to eat and drink, the psychological effect was quite what I used to get from taking communion in the Methodist Church. And both are quite comparable—psychologically again—to what I see on the faces of Catholics, Roman and Anglican, returning from the altar after communicating.

As Augustine recognized, every traditional religion, true or false, has had its visible signs or sacraments. If he thus generalized the term, we have every right to continue doing so.

The essence of symbolism or sacramentalism, from our point of view, is that, not a legal or metaphysical pattern on the curtain conveys the designs and the properly allocated potency of the tremendum but that all of this is tangibly represented in an outward and visible sign, form, object, or act. Many years ago, a physician, member of a sect which puts extreme emphasis on immersion in baptism, said to me of the rite:

> It was a business proposition. I knew when I stood on one side of the baptismal pool that I was damned to hell, but that, if I went down into the water and was baptized, I would be saved in heaven. It was a business proposition; I went in.

Theologians rarely use such unvarnished language to describe a sacrament as having efficacy *ex opere operato,* but the doctor's words express exactly the function and appeal of sacraments and symbols. I once repeated the story of the doctor's baptism to a Catholic priest with whom I happened to ride on a train. He chuckled at it, waved his hand deprecatingly, and said, "Superstition, superstition"; then he added, "But I know exactly how he felt."

Sacraments have inherent power, even though the person partaking of them may not comprehend them at all, as in the case of First Communion, given long before a child could have the least understanding (though he might prattle the phrases) of what the Eucharist implies and still more as in the baptismal regeneration of infants. I have written elsewhere at such length and with so much sympathy about the value of symbols that I may speak of them only briefly here.

Symbols and sacraments really belong together, as comes vividly to mind when we recall that "symbol" is not only the word for a potent object, such as the cross, a "holy picture," or the Torah scroll, but also for "the outward signs of the sacrament," as the *Catholic Encyclopedia* says of the Eucharist (*s.v.* "Symbolism"). Interpretation of the symbol may go as far as to declare explicitly that the symbol actually *is* the holy Reality, as with the elements in the Eucharist, or that the presence of that Reality may be only implicitly felt in the symbol, as in an image of the Virgin or of the Buddha. An intelligent Buddhist will no more admit that he is worshiping the symbol than will an intelligent Catholic admit direct worship of a picture of the Sacred Heart. But both prefer to do their devotions before the symbol because the symbol seems actually to bring the great Reality to them in a worshipful form or, as the priest on the train more conservatively expressed it to me, stimulates their piety.

Some religious traditions encourage approaches to the great Reality through symbolic acts or objects as others do not, and we have seen how people like to call the use of symbols that are strange to them "superstition" or "idolatry." Yet, if we are forced to endure long periods of horror, we tend to be like the men in the trenches of the first World War and in the foxholes of the second, when soldiers of all faiths would go to the Catholic chaplains for medals or crosses. Reconciliation with the tremendum through symbols may take the most primitive form or be developed into as profoundly rational and beautiful a thing as the High Mass. The Mass itself, however, does not affect the Catholic primarily through the understanding. Although the communicant is urged to prepare by reading and contemplation so that he will comprehend the depths and heights of the sacrament, when he actually communicates he is taught to stop all that, hold his intellectual as well as his physical powers in abeyance, and quietly open his heart as he does his mouth to receive the Reality. A person not brought up to do this from childhood can rarely learn thus to concentrate his devotions and reverence through a blessed object or rite or, shall I say, bring his mind to focus through a symbolic lens. But we cannot understand the religious patterns of the vast majority of people all over the world without seeing that human piety is almost everywhere thus directed. Even the nonsymbolic Moslem has his prayer rug, his mihrab, and his Mecca.

The Church

It may seem strange to discuss the church as a type of religious formulation apart from symbols and sacraments, but actually, though both are so important in formal religions, each may appear without the other, and inherently they involve quite different psychological values. If one wants to combine the two on the ground that the church is only a distinct sort of symbol, I have no objection. But the social and collective implications of an organization are so unlike those of such a symbol as the cross or the rosary that we gain understanding by treating them separately. All religions offer at least some symbols, and organization appears in every society, usually as we have said in discussing legalism, with a more or less clearly recognized divine sanction.

Just as religious symbols become indistinguishable from such "secular" symbols as the flag, so we shall find no clear division between church and state. Certainly medieval thinkers could hardly agree where one began and the other stopped. From out point of view, the medieval conflict between church and state was one between two churches, since the protagonists of each insisted that their great organizations brought divine will, knowledge, and rulership into the world.

The church, as we shall discuss it, is to be taken as a corporate body, superior to the individual, itself the medium of revelation, in which the individual can find divine guidance, protection, and the means of grace. It at once minimizes the individual by subordinating him to the larger entity and enlarges him by his sense of membership in it. The curtain between the individual and the tremendum becomes a corporate body. Obedience to the hierarchy of priest, bishop, and pope; of that from *Gauleiter* to *Führer*; from corporal to general; or from ward heeler to the state or national directors of party organization takes the place of a code of behavior, creed, or theology. The good for man is good for the church, and "churchman" often means no more than a person dedicated to the organization, as is the good Nazi, Communist, soldier, or party member. Let me repeat, all these terms may mean much more than this, so that the bishop who is *only* a churchman appears rarely. But the type is common enough to be quite familiar, both in leaders and followers.

In extreme form, churchmen actually profess that the church is the body or the bride of Christ whose operations are so intimately guided and controlled by God that there is "no salvation" in this life or the next outside it. There have recently been some modifications of this position by the Catholic Church to relieve tensions created by the existence of Jews, Protestants, and Hindus (and many others) of the highest character. Extraecclesiastical early training may admittedly so condition a person that he may have a psychological block against recognizing the Church for what it really is, may have "invincible ignorance" (the Church's name for it), and a merciful God will take this into the ultimate reckoning. A Presbyterian president of a college once said to a student, "I have known a few good Methodists." Such rare and rather unaccountable aberrations by no means affect the basic thinking of the churchman, Southern Democrat, Northern Republican, Communist, or Nazi that salvation comes from membership in and obedience to the one true and proper organization. Even the diplomatic corps of a country has to be structured according to exactly this acceptance of orders from one's superiors. And, of course, a bank or business corporation! At this point, one seems to have got a long way from religion, but only at first and not psychologically. When loyalty to the organized group becomes a man's supreme loyalty, before which his other scales of values, his other codes, his private judgments become secondary, then he has become a churchman, whatever his church may be called. One is often a loyal churchman as both an Episcopalian and a Republican, but such an appearance of polytheism will not surprise us. It is the "organization man" as a religious type that we are considering.

We have here again, obviously, another blueprint type of religion, a type resting on assurance through something given. It is, oddly, a phenomenon chiefly manifest in Western religious attitudes. Even Islam, strongly as its members feel united, has never organized itself as a church, whereas Hinduism and Buddhism even approximate organization only within certain orders of monks. How much it appears in more savage religions, I cannot say. Even the mystery religions of the ancient world, though intensely sacramental and hence with priests to administer the initiations, never became churches in the sense in which we are here using the term. But, in our civilization, it has played such a tremendous part, as it still does, that we must rank its importance very high.

Conversion

The experience of conversion differs from those we have been discussing in that it is a temporary one, rather than an over-all adjustment. When the earlier students of the psychology of religion were writing, conversion played so important a part in the Protestantism which largely surrounded them that they gave it considerable attention. Psychologically, we might now describe that sort of conversion in terms of a surrender of the id to the highest social relation, that with Christ, and a consequent reorientation of the entire personality. The previous attitude had been one of assent to the idea that Christ, the ideal, should properly rule in the soul, but the id so asserted its drive for gratification that the assent was largely formal. The guilt felt within the soul was a mild or severe beating administered by the drive for social security through social adjustment. Before conversion, the individual had developed a measure of tolerance for this beating, though it might register as diffused anxiety. The conduct against which the conscience, as we may still call the social drive, was protesting might have been only a "worldly life" in general, an interest in people, athletics, business, a good time, which produced an indifference to theological matters or to the highest social reality of God. But it might also center in more actually "sinful acts, such as alcoholism or forbidden sexual indulgences (with adolescents, often masturbation). Indulgence would be followed by remorse, but soon the person would again indulge. Conversion was usually induced when a preacher stimulated this anxiety into guilt or even terror by vividly describing God's wrath, while offering the peace of God to those who renounced the id and "surrendered" to the divine law or Savior.

The sense of guilt often had little relation to what human society would consider actual wickedness. With the "surrender," a new force seemed to enter, a new power to control, so that many helpless alcoholics, for example, could actually renounce the bottle and indeed "become new creatures in Christ Jesus." The new power was officially called "grace," but what it was and still is in terms of psychology it is fortunately not my present purpose to try to guess. With many, this experience did become a recurrent event, as when the town drunk would be converted at the "protracted" meetings each winter, only to be found again within a month in the gutter. With others, the whole life dramatically changed at once, so that the convert took on a new character and dynamic. It is interesting that only those could respond to such an appeal who were brought up with a Protestant theology, one which they had always accepted intellectually, but had rejected in practice as the id overpowered them. The Protestant missions had to send Catholics to Catholic priests for help.

Though many Catholic saints have had these experiences (one need name only Francis of Assisi and Ignatius Loyola), the Catholic churches have in general not encouraged them. They have indeed encouraged repentance for sins and "turning to God," but they have made God immediately available through the sacraments to those who sought him, rather than trusting to the individual to find grace without external help, alone with the Alone. As a technique for ministering to the mass of men, the sacraments clearly have a more steady effect than the mourners' bench at a "revival." It might be argued that each time a Catholic confesses, receives absolution, and does penance, he has had an experience of conversion and that in the sacraments the Catholic actually lives a life of conversion. Insofar as the church provides sacraments to meet the needs of the guilty individual, it might be argued, it offers a blueprint in place of the individual creative experience. But to follow this through would add little to what has been said about the sacraments and would be largely the sort of terminological discussion I am trying to avoid.

Conversions in other senses are similarly transitional. When a person accepts a new body of ideas, what I might call a new design on his curtain, as when a Jewish student of mine in Asia became a Buddhist, the transition does not involve guilt. In this sense, a person can be converted away from a religion as well as to it; apostasy, the rejection of a faith, is conversion no less than acceptance. Any type of conversion may be sudden or gradual.

Mysticism

In many of the experiences we have discussed, especially in the creative ones, a tendency has appeared to identify oneself with the object, a tendency to mysticism. Through art, the poet or musician, at least during his creative periods, participates in the beauty he envisages and tries to express. In general, the blueprint religions can be distinguished from the creative in that they are horizontal paths, rather than vertical ones. They show a man "the way he should go," how he should act in legalism, believe in orthodoxy, feel according to given artistic conventions, obey in the church. But always the most devout people have gone beyond these patterns; they have identified themselves with the sources of the patterns and so have risen above the human path of conformity.

In discussing sacraments and conversion, we discovered a new dimension, one in which the individual tries to transcend human limitations and assimilate divine nature into himself or himself into divine nature. When this vertical dimension enters and the individual wants not merely to conform to given standards, but to take into himself the Reality behind those standards, we say that the person's religious pattern has become mystical. Psychologically, the blueprint religions, those of the horizontal path, seem to continue the ideal life of the boy with his father, the life of acceptance and being accepted, of conformity and obedience. The vertical path, as we shall see, much more suggests the infant's relation with the mother.

In mysticism, sexes become figurative and extraordinarily mixed. Indeed, the mystic commonly expresses himself in terms of overtly sexual relationships. The nun who is the "Bride of Christ" expresses herself in language a child would not use, but the relationship is essentially the Freudian one of the little girl who is fully accepted by her father, rather than of her having become Jesus' "better half." Or the relationship can be expressed in terms of a brother–sister liaison, as in the Song of Songs, a relation which the soul as female says is to be consummated "in my mother's house, who would instruct me."

Initiations frequently take the candidate through a death into a new life when he wears the garb of the god to show that he is now identified with the god, but the death is only the death of the human personality, while a new person appears when the initiate is reborn as the god. Similarly, we "die with Christ" in baptism that we may "live with him," but it is not "I" that live, but Christ that "liveth in me." Hence, "for me, to live is Christ." These phrases of Paul which we have considered can be made more abstract, or more directly vivid according to one's taste and way of thinking. There is almost no figure or mixture of figures too bizarre to appear in mystical language. The nature religion of many such peoples as the ancient Greeks used the phallus as a direct symbol of the hope of union, to which the Japanese occasionally add the vulva. For the abstract thinker, these could symbolize the forces of nature manifest in the fertility of the fields, but for the simple peasant they would more literally be the organs of the spirit or spirits in his own field. He would feel identified with this spirit, and the clearest and fullest identification for him was to revere the phallus of the field, in whose life he himself lived. Japanese rites in which dancers tie the divine phallus to themselves recall similar rites in ancient Greece.

Our tradition follows the Jewish reticence in such matters, which Greco-Roman civilization also increasingly developed. Not only have we no rituals of actual intercourse, but we make no allusions to sexual organs of Deity. They do not appear directly even in the Song of Songs, in spite of the numerous other anatomical references. But there can be no misunderstanding of what was to occur between the loving brother and sister in the mother's tent of the Song of Songs, though many Christian writings, for example the poems of St. John of the Cross, stop barely short of the overt. This sort of approach to religious experience has appeared all over the world, even, we note, in legalistic Judaism itself, for scholars are generally agreed that, whatever the background of the Song of Songs may have been, the rabbis who made the canon of the Old Testament with such scrupulous concern could never have included that book unless it had long been understood in terms of mystical allegory.

In a theistic religion, where God is personal, mysticism

expresses itself in personal ways. The Christian mystic no longer takes Christ merely as his guide, or benefits by the Passion, or even is simply "washed in His blood." The mystic must go beyond and live with Christ, in Christ, "take on Christ," or, like, Paul come to say: "For me, to live is Christ." Frank identification of oneself with the divine person is, however, too difficult even for most people with mystical inclinations. As Deity is considered more vividly in personal terms, it seems increasingly impertinent for the worshiper to claim identity or even to suggest personal relations on terms remotely suggesting identification. If Paul could say, "not I live, but Christ liveth in me," most devout Christians know very well what Paul meant, but they prefer to keep the statement within quotation marks.

Popular mysticism directed to a personal deity, accordingly, more naturally expresses itself in terms of a return to the mother. Our deepest emotional patterns are set in childhood, and, however much we may feel with Paul that we have "put away childish things," we never do so entirely. Of course we revolt from our parents as individuals, but much of our later lives can be explained only as a nostalgic reconstruction of the consolations they gave us as young children.

That is a thesis I cannot here debate. To those who think that they have run from such consolations, all I can say is that the little boy running away from his mother or having a tantrum of rebellion on the floor is quite as much a child as the tot who walks down the street clutching his mother's skirt. I have come to understand adults far more deeply as I have come to understand and respect young children.

So it is not strange to me that Christians very early began to direct their petitions more to the Mother of God than to either the Father or Son and that Clement of Alexandria should have aspired to "suck the breasts of God the Father."

We can identify ourselves with the child in the Virgin's arms, and it is no chance that he is properly represented and always understood as nursing at her breast. Protestants who have rejected what they call Mariolatry keep the same figure and the same confusion of sexes as did Clement of Alexandria:

> Safe in the arms of Jesus,
> Safe on his gentle breast,
> There by his love o'ershaded
> Sweetly my soul shall rest.

> I need Thee every hour.

> Do thy friends despise, forsake thee?
> Take it to the Lord in prayer;
> In His arms He'll take and shield thee,
> Thou wilt find a solace there.

> Child of weakness, watch and pray,
> Find in Me thine all in all.

> Jesus carries all our sorrow,
> Oh, how He loves.

> Savior more than life to me,
> I am clinging, clinging close to Thee.

> He leadeth me! By His own hand He leadeth me.

> Oh, to be nothing, nothing,
> Only as led by His hand.

> Jesus, lover of my soul,
> Let me to thy bosom fly.

> Draw me nearer, nearer, blessed Lord.

> Nearer, my God, to Thee.

These are the songs of deepest consolation, sung at funerals and with power even on the sinking "Titanic." They are passionate songs of nostalgia for mother-love. The Protestants who sing them *Aus tiefer Not* are not mystics in any philosophic sense, but they turn to the Great Mother, whom without confusion they call "Jesus," and in the union of the child with that Mother they find the solace of divinity.

Such a personal union normally arises through an early training which makes the divine person a vivid part of the child's life. In my Methodist boyhood, Jesus, my companion and comfort as well as my moral restraint, accompanied me quite as really as any person I lived with and much more constantly. Like Brother Lawrence, I "practiced the presence of God." [20] Later doubts about the identity of this "familiar spirit" have taken from me any confidence about its name, but have by no means left me without its attendance. How Socrates arrived at the same experience, we do not know. He simply said that there was a *daimonion* always within him guiding his life. The word in Greek was a vague one, like our "little spirit," to be qualified as "good" or "bad." But, for Socrates, to live was the *daimonion*. May we call it a vividly anthropomorphized superego, conscience, ego-ideal, or patron saint? All such terms are purely imaginative.

Whatever it is, I am convinced, quite without statistics, that a far larger proportion of men and women live with such a *daimonion*, whatever they call it or whether they call it anything at all, than is commonly suspected. Blessed is the man who, having it, lives in loving relation with it; cursed is he who lives in rebellion against it, rebuked by it, his inner life devastated by the warfare. For such a man,

[20] Nicolas Herman, *The Practice of the Presence of God* (London: 1926).

the command, "Be you reconciled with God," means quite directly to be reconciled to his *daimonion*, reconciled, not by theological explanations, though these may help some types of people, but by surrendering to it the id, the personal drive, and accepting its mother-fatherly guidance and loving support. These words will be as meaningful to some of my readers as they are utter nonsense to others. So be it.

Mysticism can go quite beyond or away from a sense of personal relation, however, and express itself in much more abstract terms. A halfway station is found in mysticisms of light, life, membership in the cosmic vine or tree, or drinking the water of life. The Hindus find it by bathing in the Ganges, a physical sacrament by which they are not only spiritually cleansed, but identify themselves with the quite extrapersonal, immaterial Reality, which is, to them, the only true Reality. The Hindus recognize the value of personal mysticism, which they experience through their personal deity, Krishna.

But beyond this is quite a different approach, in which man gradually loses his identity, not in a greater Person, but in the universal, impersonal Reality. Here the mystic must use figures to communicate, but he prefers silence, which he calls the only true philosophy, because figures must all come from the material world and because he must go beyond their inadequacy quite as much as beyond the personal. Mystic philosophy is only talking about mysticism, not the experience itself. The talking has mystical value only as it takes the mind beyond concepts to concept. So the mystic confuses figures in a way that flouts all rules of rhetoric or logic. He revels in paradox, since he must tear the mind away from the observed world of cause and effect. "The way up and the way down are the same," said Heraclitus. Male and female carry us far beyond their personal manifestation, the Cabalists taught, but even this distinction disappears in the realm of true Being from which all distinctions subtend, but in which they cease to exist.

The approach to it is universally the *via negativa*, the road of negation, in which we come to recognize that all categories and classifications are, as Philo said, illusions, false perceptions. The mystic achieves his end when every one of his own formulations lose value, and in the complete nothing of human categories he finds the all and only of reality. As Philo said, the Light of Being can come to us only when the light of human thought is extinguished. So the ultimate could be called Darkness, the Cloud of Unknowing, interchangeably with Light, or *Gnosis* (knowledge), and indeed a negative term, like the "Not so" of the East, would frequently be preferred, since it carries less physical and human connotation than do positive figures.

Few men of our civilization actively cultivate such a state, but many of us have passing moments, at least, when it comes upon us. Some of our greatest activists and commanders have to take time out, perhaps not in the trancelike contemplation of Zen monks, but in music, poetry, or some sort of relaxation in which they sense the "something far more deeply interfused." As this becomes interfused with themselves, it seems to them their source of most profound understanding, with power even to quiet and control the tumult of daily concerns.

5

Religion as Search

IN SPEAKING OF THE VARIOUS TYPES of religious experience,
I have clearly been regarding them with detachment—
though not without sympathy. Ernst Troeltsch liked to
speak of the "polymorphism" of religion, the many forms
it may take; he had in mind the diversity of the various
organized or tribal religious systems and rites of worship.
Religion is, we have seen, polymorphic from the psychological point of view as well. All organized or tribal religions have their own myths and rituals, in which there are
often common motifs and practices, and each such religion
must be considered for its distinctive god names, customs,
and the like. The psychological forms that I have discussed,
on the other hand, appear everywhere in greater or less de-

gree. One would find all the psychological types of religion here described in India, Burma, or Russia quite as easily as in New York or Paris. And we have seen that a man's religion consists of the rites, myths, principles, ideals, and objectives which in practice actually guide his life, not the ones he verbally professes.

In discussing them, I have shown less sympathy for what I have called the blueprint religions—whether the blueprint calls for legalism; orthodoxy; sacraments; traditional symbols; an organized and ancient church; or accepted forms of music, poetry, or architecture. But I have admitted that I cannot reject many of these, since they are part of my total adjustment to society and the universe, and what I am actually living by and for cannot be separated from what I must call my religion, since it *is* my religion.

When William James had finished describing the various forms which he saw in religious experience, he closed his great book by suggesting his own approach to religion. I should do the same.

My problem is not which of the old formulations one can preserve, but, starting all over again, how the modern man, who is still *Homo religiosus*, is to live in the new age of science. Granted that such a man has little use for the old myths, can he fit himself into the old psychological patterns of religious experience, or must he make a new one? We must begin with still another question, what I mean by "modern man," even though this at once takes us into further confusion. The trouble is that no modern man is wholly modern and that relatively few of our contemporaries are modern in their thinking at all. The various types of thought and emotion I have been describing and most of the old myths are for most living people as valid now as they were two thousand years ago.

When I use the term "modern man," I mean one who is adjusting his thinking and living as far as possible to the criteria of reality recognized as the best that the natural and social sciences know. His standards come not from the past —from ancient Palestine or Greece, the thirteenth century, the Elizabethan period, or the seventeenth, eighteenth, or nineteenth centuries, at least not as absolutes. Acknowledging the values in these heritages, he knows he must live in the modern world of exploding knowledge and of congealing, leveling humanity. He must not only live in it, but accept it, function as a part of it, and want to do so.

This is quite an inadequate definition, since modern artists, poets, and musicians have gone into new forms of creativity which have little reference to the old conventions. We have considered their creativity as part of the deeply valuable experience of aestheticism. But theirs is only partially a new world, since men have thought in art and music for untold centuries, and, though the conventions are now new, still the modern artist knows that he belongs much more with Phidias and Botticelli than with Newton or Einstein, more with Aeschylus and Shakespeare than with Edison. Most artists are rather shrill in saying so. Their experience is still valid, but as a basis for living in the new world of science and society it can be the experience of few of us.

The modern man, as I am using the term, is a *novum*, for not until very recent times have people felt obliged to study man and the universe by controlled and systematic investigation. Plato, Thomas Aquinas, Shakespeare, and Goethe, each in his own way, had magnificent insights, and Gibbon was indeed a historian born out of due time. But, when scientists could say a few years ago that 95 per cent of all scientists who had ever lived were then alive, we see what a new age scientists have really created.

Modern man—I think it can be said in general—has had a new vision of reality, one of seemingly endless regress in cause and effect, in time and space, and in the complications of developmental mutations. Heraclitus suggested such a world to the Greeks, but the Greeks could not face endless regress in causation. The four causes of Aristotle were typically Greek in that they had a beginning, middle, and end (at least in the sense of a goal), and thinking not thus contained was to almost all Greeks "ridiculous." From them has come the consistent urge of our philosophers and the tradition of all Western thought that we must have a first cause as well as a final cause, a sense of cosmic process with beginning and objective, in order to have a meaningful universe. Creation and purpose haunt all our thinking. In the name of modern science, a physiologist may deny with bluster, when a layman asks him, that the liver or pancreas have any "purpose," but in a physiologist's own speech the old terms or obvious substitutes for them soon reappear. Very well, let us speak of the "function" of the liver in the total organization of the body, but, in doing so, all of us, physiologists included, tend to think teleologically. "Meaning" has from the times of the Greeks been largely a teleological term, in small things and in universals. The vermiform appendix, having no essential function, is dispensable and hence meaningless. With the Greek teleology in causation, our tradition has mixed the later Jewish sense of historical time and divine plan of progress from creation to the final cosmic resolution that we usually call eschatology. As a result of either tradition or of both together, few of us can think of meaning apart from some sort of beginning and objective.

On the contrary, the world of today's science (not necessarily of tomorrow's) is the one which Heraclitus proposed, the world of perpetual mutations in fire. "The way up and the way down are the same," he said. For his primal base, fire, we might now substitute inconceivably hot hydrogen gas or subparticle electrical "energy" itself. To come to a Person or Mind behind this who created it, we must erect a ladder of mythology, or of anthropomorphic wish-projection—in whatever metaphysical polysyllables we describe it. Unlike the Greeks, a man today who cannot endure what seems to be infinite regress and mutation appears to think ridiculously and belong to past ages. A first cause and teleology both seem to have disappeared in a universe of evolution.

That is, the modern man accepts the tremendum rather than impose a mythological scheme upon it. He has curtains still, but, insofar as he is modern, he paints hypotheses on them, not "truths," and lives in this world of hypothesis—lives by hypotheses in physics, biology, personal ethics, social organization and, if he thinks about it at all, by hypotheses in metaphysics. The modern mind sees meaning in hypotheses because, when tested, they lead to better hypotheses. If you will, he is still thinking teleologically about meaning, but his test of meaning is purely pragmatic. Our "modern" leaders of popular thought, our theologians (even Tillich most of the time), poets, novelists, and playwrights, leaders of most of those who call themselves intelligentsia, regard living by hypotheses as failure and try to take us back to ultimates which are only thinly disguised traditional patterns. Or they make their living by chanting threnodies about the loss of form, purpose, and hence meaning in human life. The truly modern men are steeplejacks climbing to dangerous heights; indeed, they are mountaineers scrambling far beyond the peaks of Everest or descending into inconceivable depths. The ones who become dizzy are those who watch them from what they suppose is the real ground.

To the modern mind, there is no ground any more, no fixed level or point of meaningful reference. Such a world is not for cowards, but such is the world in which modern man lives.

If modern man sees no trace of a personal, loving God who makes all things work together for good to them who love him, there seems as little room for the God of deism, the ultimate clockmaker who created a perfect machine and then left it to run by the laws he had established. Evolution from primeval hydrogen or electric energy bears little resemblance to the running of a clock. That our reasons can discern what we call relations of cause and effect by no means indicate that a "Reason" on a cosmic scale must have established those relations. The ultimate laws of the universe seem now to be in some way inherent properties of hydrogen gas or of the electric energy of which that gas is composed. Granted that we live in a world guided by eternal laws, as many scientists do not grant, nothing demands that we posit a lawmaker. We must, like the Greeks, stop our recess in thinking somewhere, but there is no more difficulty in making electric energy with inherent characteristics our final stop than in making it a Mind that has inherent power and characteristics. The little child who asks, "But who made God?", senses at once that "God" is also an arbitrary stopping-point. Science stops with the electric energy, theism or deism with God; the former with a hypothesis, the latter with a dogma.

In science, "law" is simply a human term for the properties of the ultimate substrate, a figure of speech from human categories. When contemporary theologians say that the business of man is to find his "relation to God's purposes," we are not in the modern world at all. In this matter, the philosophers of the East have far less adjustment to make than do we Westerners, since they never put a person in place of the ultimate impersonal substrate of Brahma or Nirvana. With them in mind, however, it at once emerges that, if science has left us no reason to presuppose a divine mind and person, it has not thereby cut us off from religion, since those who have reconciled themselves to the ultimate in terms of Brahma or Nirvana could hardly be called irreligious. Perhaps we do not want to use these Oriental terms ourselves, and I personally see no reason why we should use them. But they do show at once that religion can flourish profoundly without a personal mind or purpose of God.

As we saw in discussing mysticism, we need not go to the East for such an approach at all. The Western tradition of mysticism itself assumes that the ultimate is something quite beyond human categories; beyond what we can conceive as goodness, justice, or any other human characteristic; beyond even what we can understand as being itself. Our deepest religious spirits have gone to such an ultimate by the *via negativa* quite as completely as have the Eastern mystics to the "Not So." When the ultimate has become the Ineffable, the Indescribable, the Incommunicable, the Darkness that is Light, we have actually a set of terms which we can use in the modern world without hesitation, since they indicate a direct acceptance of the tremendum as such. The contemporary name for this way of thinking is "agnosticism," and the term, along with its practitioners, is as much disliked by modern theologians as were the mystics and pietists of Judaism and Christianity by the religious doctrinaires. To me, "agnosticism" is only the contemporary word to express one's acceptance of the fact that we do not know the reality in which we live. Any given agnostic may or may not be a mystic in the sense that he has an immediate feeling of union with the tremendum. Like most religious spirits of the past, he may well be content with lesser observances and details of the law. But his feeling that the universe calls for no personal creator or ruler by no means cuts him off from the company of the devout.

We may well have reverence before or as a part of a universe seemingly without beginning or end and certainly with no apparent teleological purpose. Insofar, however, as we cling to the dream of a "far-off divine event to which the whole creation moves" and call the new universe of process meaningless because it does not correspond to antiquated criteria of meaning, we disqualify ourselves for living fully in that universe. In such a case, the trouble is not with the new world, but with our inherited limitations of "meaning." These limitations are really the bath water that may well be thrown down the drain.

Most of man's dreams of teleology have centered on a sort of tragicomic ending in which man himself is the victorious hero, for we have inherited a homocentric view of the universe along with a God-created view. In the Judeo-Christian tradition, creation culminated in man himself, who had been made in God's image to be his companion on walks in the Garden of Eden. The rest of the universe was only a sort of backdrop for man. I cannot believe that people remove themselves from religion when they can no longer believe that the universe must find its highest achievement and goal in the human race. For modern man, the homocentric cosmos has disappeared as completely as the geocentric. As we now see that men have their gods in their own image, so we recognize that homocentrism is only egocentrism writ large. On the contrary, biologists are quite prepared to discover that cosmic evolution has produced forms of life far superior to what man has become on this earth and that, on some remote planet of some remote sun, there may be "people" as much superior to Homo sapiens as man considers himself above the snake or toad.

Is it then possible for man to have a sense of meaning,

value, and purpose for mankind if he must accept himself as a relatively late form of mutation in the great flux of hydrogen or electric energy, a mutation whose survival definitely depends on this planet's enduring under conditions fairly well established in their present form? Perhaps a billion years hence—which seems now the most optimistic hope for such duration—men will have become clever enough to transport themselves to another heavenly body where they can continue when this planet is no longer habitable. But we know nothing of this and may ourselves hope nothing from it. To all appearances, anything we would call a human being began to exist only a million years ago, and sooner or later the race will be totally reabsorbed in the flux.

Furthermore, though not denying the possibility, the modern mind sees no reason whatever to suppose that we as individuals have immortal souls which emerge from their corporate affiliations at death and find meaning at last in some sort of eternal life. The utterly unexplained "spark of life" seems no more eternal in man than in the mosquito. The Indian or Buddhist accepts that and says that life is eternal in both. That is the picture or one of them on their curtain. The West has made the absurd distinction that the life of man implies eternity, but that that of the pig does not. That is our picture. Modern biology cannot explain the nature and origin of life in either man or pig, but sees no basis for the distinction in man's favor. Biologically, human death seems exactly like animal death and in each case involves the extinction of the individual. We live and die biologically. Whatever life is, it seems to be a function of the body. The body outlasts its own life, but only briefly; it soon decays and returns to the flux. Even the Bible recognized "dust to dust."

It would be absurd to assert that this is the final truth

about life and death; but that it is the sober opinion of modern science, its best present conclusion, is common knowledge. Faith has been well defined as a belief which is not altered or shaken by evidence to the contrary. Modern man can hardly make a virtue of faith in that sense. True, personal immortality for human beings has not been disproved, and many find belief in it extremely consoling. In these matters, however, modern man does not ask for proof before he gives up his fantasies; rather, admitting that he does not fully know, he accepts as his working hypothesis what seems from the evidence the most probable explanation. If life is to have any meaning for modern man, therefore, it must be within the universe and in terms of the best scientific understanding we can get. We must, I shall soon point out, go beyond such knowledge, but never against it.

Historical techniques, in the second place, come in to make modern man's predicament still more stark. More than a century ago, it was made clear that we have no evidence that Moses or Jesus broke through the order of nature to reveal to man a supernatural dimension of existence. The modern historian feels not the slightest obligation to prove that there was no such revelation; he simply says that no evidence exists by the accepted canons of historical judgment to establish that there was one. Historians can also find no period in the past when men as a whole were less cruel, avaricious, lecherous, and shallow than now. Great individuals have indeed appeared, before whose courage and wisdom we feel utterly inferior, and on rare occasions, such as in Athens at its height or in the days of the founders of the American republic, to name only two, several such geniuses appeared simultaneously. But these were all men of their time, and their teachings stultify us when taken as literally authoritarian truth for later generations. The new theologians confuse every issue when they try to revive the authority of the Bible as a revelation of final truth, however "demythologized," and insist that man is helpless, perverted, lost, unless saved in Jesus Christ.

This is no place to discuss my own basic scholarly interest, the problem of the origins of Christianity. There is no more reason, historically, to doubt that Jesus of Nazareth existed, that he was crucified, and that a large number of his followers thought that they saw him alive after his death than to doubt the existence of Socrates. But the incarnate Logos, the Second Adam, and the like, have no claim to historical credibility whatever. Spiritual exaltation arising from such beliefs establishes their truth no more than a child's delight in Santa Claus proves the genial saint's reality. The whole structure of thinking of Jesus and his followers in the early church assumes God's personality; man's centrality in God's interest; the three-story universe of hell, earth, and heaven; and God's special act in a divine historical event that changed the whole course of man's relation to the ultimate.

What, we ask, is a historical fact or event? Many things have happened which have disappeared from human recollection or recall. Despite its generally loose usage, the word "history" carries a precise meaning to historians: a historic event is an inference which experts unite in drawing after examining the data which attest it. So all people who have studied the records agree that Columbus crossed the Atlantic in 1492 and that Washington crossed the Delaware on Christmas Eve, 1776.

Many incidents occurred in connection with these events, incidents not recorded and so not a part of history. At the same time, many legends have grown up and been told as history, such as that of Washington and the cherry tree, only to be shown later to have no adequate support in evidence, not to be justifiable inference, and hence not historical fact. The historian cannot say that Washington did not cut down the cherry tree; he can only say that there is no adequate evidence that he did so, and, accordingly, whether he did or not, it cannot be called a historical fact. As historians, we must assume that it did not happen, however much we may like the story.

Similarly, historians are not in a position to deny that Jesus was the son of God as related in the Christmas stories, but they do say that the evidence has by no means convinced the majority of them beyond reasonable doubt that he was so. Without such evidence, historians can no more pronounce an event historical, a fact, than can a jury without sufficient evidence pronounce a man guilty of a crime, however much they may suspect his guilt. The historian cannot use as the basis of life's meaning a story from or about the past which has no evidence to support it.

The historian does, indeed, see great events and periods in the past, such as classical Athens, the Hebrew prophets, the Buddha, Confucius—all amazingly contemporary with one another. The later beginnings of Christianity and Islam and the Renaissance in Europe and England were also cataclysmic events in the great flux of human life. But the historian has no more need of divine intervention to explain them than has the astronomer to explain a *novum*. Actually, neither the historian nor the astronomer can explain these occurrences. Ignorance only whets the appetite for greater understanding—of human nature in the one case and of astrophysics in the other. It does not suggest to either the historian or the astronomer that he put unfounded fancies, however clever, into the gaps of his knowledge. This is what modern history forces on modern man.

As man has been losing his authoritative accounts of existence and life's purpose, modern sociology and anthropology, in the third place, have cut in to show that the frameworks of social right and wrong in which men found security have likewise for the most part turned out to be pragmatic local adjustments. The inherent holiness of life itself, especially human life, is one of the highest aspects of human ethics, but is a major premise which, if it be allowed to lead us to prohibit birth control, may turn the world into a Black Hole of Calcutta, where humanity stifles itself. If a modern state is to survive at all, we are increasingly learning, the sanctity of private property must be invaded by all sorts of confiscations, which we dignify by the term "taxes." What would be the "right" regulations for property, sex, the education of children, labor relations, or any of the other "bulwarks of society"? Here, again, we see that almost every conceivable system of adjustment has been tried in one place or another, and each has been regarded as "right" so long and only so long as it accomplished what men wanted from it. When old adjustments were kept after their usefulness had ceased, as with the aristocracy of declining Rome, the civilization crumbled. "One good custom" has corrupted many civilizations. In social ethics, we seem to be back in the endless permutations and combinations of the cosmic flux. The price of development seems again to be change, destruction, and frequent failure. This, too, modern man must accept. He may have reservations about the feasibility of many suggested changes, but a sense of final social and ethical orthodoxy has no place in the new world or in a modern man's thinking. Loyalty to the best ethical and political practice we know, along with adaptability to new conditions—these are the difficult necessities for modern man.

Much as we have been saying about psychology in this book, we must return to say a few more words about some of the problems it presents to us which we have not yet mentioned. Man has always been perplexed about himself and his motives, but now the experimental psychologists put us completely into the natural process of cause and effect by demonstrating that, to an alarming extent if not entirely, man is an automaton formed by his experiences, one who responds to new situations in what would be, if we had all the evidence, quite predictable ways. At the same time, the depth psychologists see man as almost as fully conditioned and formed by early experiences, whose meaning is buried far down in the unconscious, which the individual can never understand or control. Or, if we recognize individual differences from birth, we tend to understand these in terms of genes, about which the individual can do nothing. In all this, the deeply important conception of moral responsibility seems to vanish, for, if we have no choice or freedom, we can hardly be called responsible. Can life have meaning if we have no power to direct our thoughts, motives, or actions?

I have stated the claim of determinism in a purposely exaggerated form, since there is indeed much such talk going about. Elizabeth Beardsley,[1] for example, has recently urged that, since the feelings of moral judgment ". . . cannot be rationally justified, human beings had better try to eliminate them from their psyches as soon as possible. The fact that there is no reason to believe that this has ever been accomplished is not likely to daunt . . ." such thinkers. Mrs. Beardsley has here overplayed the rationalist's hand. In fact, no feelings can be rationally justified, but the feeling of the importance of responsibility for our actions, since our whole

[1] "Determinism and Moral Perspectives," *Philosophy and Phenomenological Research*, XXI (1960), 5.

structure of law in society is based on it, has at least considerable pragmatic justification. Actually, our emotions exist whether we justify them rationally or not, and to suppose that we can dispose of them by rational argument, eliminate them for our psyches, stretches our imagination far more than the idea that there may be something wrong in the assumption of total determinism.

All research in experimental psychology, all clinical probing of a patient's psyche by an analyst, all research in genes, must be done in terms of seeking causes for present attitudes, behavior, or conditions. This is an inevitable working hypothesis, and it has brought, is bringing, a new psychic world into view—or, rather, bits of the new world, so that we recall Dobzhansky's remark: "A common foible of scientists is to suppose that the little truths they discover explain everything rather than something." [2] Still less can we take our working hypotheses to be facts so universal and established that we can eliminate from our psyches evidence to the contrary. I have taught too many thousands of young men not to know that the one thing needful to make a scholar is an inner drive, obsession, along with an individual power to make inductive leaps which no amount of teaching, drilling, or conditioning could ever instill.

Psychologists still have a long way to go to establish a simple cause-and-effect relation between Shakespeare's experiences as a boy in Stratford and his later creativity or between Hitler's youthful frustrations and his later almost-cosmic enormities. From the point of view of experimentation or therapy, we have to operate on the hypothesis of psychic determinism. But, without a sense of moral judgment, of individual creativity, integrity, and reality, we would indeed have a problem on our hands. In a word, even

[2] Theodosius Dobzhansky, "Man Consorting with the Eternal," in Harlow Shapley, ed., *Science Ponders Religion* (New York: 1960), p. 134.

if man ultimately has no freedom, he must assume that he has it and act on the assumption if he is to be a human being. No one demonstrates this more clearly than the scientist himself who refuses to accept generalizations as facts until they are demonstrated. To reserve judgment is to exercise freedom of judgment. How this sense of freedom emerged in man from within the great flux I cannot say nor, at this stage, can anyone. But a sense of responsibility is not only the zest but the nerve of life.

Herein, perhaps, the advantage of reserving judgment becomes clear. We must accept the findings of science, but accept the present limitations of science as well. If science has gone so far that men can deal successfully with sub-atomic energy and shoot a rocket to photograph the moon, clearly we must admit this world of fact. The three-story universe and the mythology that went with it have gone forever, as has any idea that history attests an event or events wherein supernatural reality was revealed. Man has nothing but his desires to support his believing in immortality, either for himself or for the race.

Yet man the essential baby does have an extraordinary zest for living, for doing, for knowing, as well as an urge for aggression and destruction of others, along with an urge for cooperation and peace. Man the vital animal is still the greatest fact of our experience, and, if we are to be realists, we must begin and end in it. I am by no means recommending that we consider ours a euphoric existence in the best of all possible worlds, but I definitely do say that what carries us through our depressions (and I know them as well as anyone not in psychotic melancholia) is precisely this vital urge. It is this urge which has given man what little knowledge he has, as well as made him "a biological success despite the tragic discords within his own soul." But to be a man, we now see, means to endure these discords and to refuse to try to escape them by resorting to simple explanations. An illusion that science has now explained all things is not only to misunderstand science totally, but to paint a curtain of myth again. Clarity and honesty can be found only as we admit our limitations and, I still insist, continue to accept responsibility for what we must still call our decisions. The test of modern maturity is the ability to tolerate paradox and question marks, to accept the unknown as unknown, to adjust to the universe of flux and our apparently minuscule place in it.

Our real question here, however, is how modern man can be religious in this new world. Have we ceased to be *Homines religiosi?* Is the religious experience an illusion because its traditional structures and explanations have been such?

I do not see that that follows at all. I and many of my friends have found that we need not deny any of what seems to be reality in order to live deeply religious lives. We do not create new certainties; the ages of certainty took their last stand on the theory of the atom as ultimate and burst into startling uncertainty when the power within the atom was released. The age when men thought deductively from an over-all Prime or "ground of being" has given way to a world which we can approach only by piecemeal investigation. Thoughtful men are now more deeply concerned with the tremendous than ever before—concerned to study the tremendum itself, not to make up fanciful stories about it. A new understanding will be the formulation of a new "law" of physics or biology or of a new conception of the meaning of some period in history. On the basis of this understanding, "applied scientists" can in turn have a vivid experience of the tremendum as they use the work of the theorists to make bridges, aircraft, or long tunnels under water or, as doctors, to heal the sick. We might call them the blueprint practitioners of the religion of quest.

The creative theorists, however, actually put on the curtains quite new patterns, if only small details. Many scientific theorists have told me as much, and as a historian I would say the same of historical reconstructions. George Wald, the great biologist, once said to me: "We used to answer questions with answers. Now we answer them with questions." The "law" is itself a projection on the tremendum or, rather, on the curtain that still screens the tremendum from us. When we call it "law," it is a projection; when we call it a hypothesis, it is much less so, not so at all in the old sense of the projections. The law of gravity, for example, is a human description of how masses seem to relate to one another. It is derived by induction from observed phenomena—scientific induction, if you will. It is a good and useful working hypothesis to put on our curtains, because its results are far more predictable, within its limits, than the results of prayer. But it is not nature itself. Einstein expressed this strikingly when he said that the only thing incomprehensible about the universe was that it was comprehensible. That is, it is incomprehensible that the thinking in our funny little heads should so correspond to reality that preventive serums and astronomical predictions are possible. We have even this accuracy, of course, only in piecemeal observations. Knowing how little of the universe he did comprehend, Einstein would never have said this had he not spoken from a profound reverence for the still-unknown, along with a triumphant faith in the quest and man's intelligence. He was a deeply religious man of the quest.

Indeed, Einstein was one of the great pioneers, prophets, of the religion of the quest, though his religious pronouncements came out only rarely. Personally, the scientist expects that at death he will of course be dissolved back into the tremendum, but he alleviates what distresses others in the prospect as he comes to understand even a small part of the unknown about and within him. He really does come to control the otherwise-uncontrollable, to explain the hitherto-inexplicable, if only an insignificant fraction of it. Insofar as he thus adjusts to the tremendum, he has a religious experience. The scientist, like Paul, counts himself not to have attained and presses on toward an ever-receding mark. It is a religious experience for both alike.

Replicas of the older patterns continue in this otherwise-novel religious adjustment. The creative scholar is always a man of faith, faith in the age-old tenet that the truth will set us free. Because he prizes truth so highly, he devotes his life to finding it. Only the method differs, important as that difference is. Scholars would be the first to protest that, unlike Ernesto Cardinal Ruffini, they can make no claim whatever to knowing "the" truth. But they are fully aware that scientists today have in many respects far more of it than men had in any previous generation. So they have faith in their method, and they have the stability that faith brings.

Modern men also have faith in man. In contrast to the traditional "there is no health in us," scientists and historians find man a rather wonderful creature whose incredible advance from the protozoon or from hydrogen gas arouses breathless admiration. The raw forces of selfishness and crime are only still-uncontrolled manifestations of the raw forces that have created man and on which he still depends. In an attempt at sounding profound, a recent book reviewer has suggested that illusion may be the only real thing in a world that is otherwise meaningless flux, horror, and chaos. Of course, we must at this stage live largely on illusions, as I have repeatedly said, and I am in no position to assert that the world is not horror. In fact, in calling it "the tremendum," as I have been doing throughout, I have been insisting that we must recognize, at this stage of our knowledge, that the world is flux. But that the world is chaos is precisely what the scientist is finding it is not. The chaos was in the head of the reviewer, as of so many such modern literati. Our knowledge of the universe soon runs into chaotic fragmentation, but that describes our ignorance, not the universe.

Man has developed through lust, robbery, and murder. These still guide us as we procreate, use the products of nature for ourselves, destroy the germs that would destroy us, and kill the animals we need for food or, in the perversity of the ages, as we slaughter the human enemies who would demolish us because they want our goods or servitude, or because we want theirs, or because their illusions about reality or social organization differ from ours. However much we may deplore the vagaries of these brute forces within us, we should be idle engines without their explosive power. But that is far from chaos.

We have returned to the Greek awareness that virtue is knowledge—not rote knowledge but such knowledge as we have that, if we touch a hot stove, we will be burned. Virtue is not knowledge of an illusion, of the traditional myths of revelation, or of the theological "means of salvation" from our wicked natures. Like the Greeks, we think that a knowledge that can produce virtue will be knowledge of ourselves, of our whole natures, individually and collectively; and we must know better the place of man in his natural surroundings and the nature of the forces that control us. If we ever have such knowledge, it will be by studying more and more carefully the smaller things. For this, the scientist must continue to have faith in his methods. Perhaps such faith is itself faith in an illusion, but the achievements of modern science are rather impressive. The scientist here stands on the old wholesome proverb of the Epistle of

James: "Faith without works is dead. I will show you my faith by my works."

It would not do, however, to give the impression that only the pure scientist is a modern man and that the religious attitude I have been describing is beyond most of us. Here my contrast between the creative and the blueprint approaches to religious experience comes in. On most subjects, we must all adjust to the tremendum by accepting the hypotheses of other thinkers. the blueprints they give us. When astronomers put definitions of distances in terms of light years, let alone billions of light years, I can repeat the words but my imagination and comprehension go blank. I am forced back to the tremendum. This I have done emotionally, but intellectually I have been given a new symbol of the tremendum to put on my curtain. Like all my forebears, I adjust to Reality, the tremendum, by using a symbol that I take on faith. I adjust in humility and reverence and joy at new learning—all of them religious attitudes. The biologist is just as much impressed by a really judicious use of evidence to reconstruct history, for the historian, too, presents only a likely hypothesis.

At last it has emerged that the metaphor of the curtains with their patterns is only a colorful way of talking about symbols. We do not think *things*, as I said about the apple, but symbols—words or forms which call to mind the material object. In physics and religion, it is as in language: we can think of reality, think at all, not by the things themselves, but by symbols for them. Years ago, my three-year-old son on his first morning with a new fourteen-year-old German *Mädchen* had a heated argument with her as to whether the thing hanging down from the end of his hobby horse was a tail or a *Schwanz*. Fortunately, the *Mädchen* won out, and with two words for the object the lad had his first lesson in linguistics and in the difference between a symbol and the reality. In Moscow, I was later much less successful when I tried to convince an intelligent young Marxist that "materialism," which he proudly said he was living by, was itself an abstraction and not the material objects themselves. The word "symbol" is the word of mathematicians for their devices in dealing with the unknown. Fantastically as the symbols of mathematics can now be applied to atomic bombs and computers and organic cells, the scientists themselves know that they are using only symbols.

In fields where we are not creative, we must just take and use the symbols creative thinkers give us. We may use them in applied science, use the interpretations of historians in fields other than ours to help us understand our own subjects, or we may accept them as blueprints to allay our timidities before the tremendum. Utterly different as they are from traditional paintings on the curtains, such as a crucifix, Shiva, or the Buddha, or from such great words as "Allah" or "Yahweh" or as the word "God" in England and America, the use or creation of these hypotheses as symbols can still give men consolation and meaning. The new way of curtaining which uses hypotheses as symbols does, indeed, make the old symbols quite meaningless to most modern men. But it offers no threat to religious life itself, whether on the creative or on the blueprint level. As the *Homo religiosus*, man may and must still live by the symbols which seem to him to give meaning to the tremendum and, in giving it meaning, take away its terror. This is not a new phenomenon. The Catholic has no use for an image of Shiva; the Hindu, none for a shophar. All of us, especially in the West, reject other people's symbols. Modern man is not irreligious because he has no use for traditional symbols; he is still religious because he still envisages and utilizes the tremendum through symbols and quiets the terror which the tremendum would arouse in him if he had no symbol-painted curtains.

Can people with this approach express themselves in worship? Certainly not in traditional forms of worship. A gathering of scientists to praise and pray to the Reality they envisage is unthinkable. A body of psychologists would never open their meeting with such a farce of prayer as does the United States Senate, but would simply plunge into earnest discussions of the latest discoveries or hypotheses about some aspect of reality with a seriousness that registers in a sacred code of honesty. Such meetings of scholars in all the fields we have discussed constitute their collective worship, one from which they return to their studies or laboratories for genuine private continuance of the search which they shared at the meeting. Prayer for modern man is replaced by eager search, which is a form of prayer itself. This is obviously an ideal picture—but so are the hopes of what may be done to Catholics in a eucharistic conference. I dare guess that the percentage of true devotion among scholars would rank very high in any general average.

So far as social ethics go, the honesty of scholars is almost unique. Their desire for recognition and fame (they are really human) may actually ruin them, as it did the pathetic hero of C. P. Snow's *The Search*, a work whose ending the scholars I know pronounce shocking. But we are all mixed up in one way or another.

In fact, few scientists and scholars are the cold, inhuman abstractions of popular imagination. Scholars have as many emotional facets, as many personal problems, as anyone else, and our total lives will involve many of the complicated adjustments which constitute religion in general. The scholar, too, is usually a polytheist. He has his adjustments to social life through legalism. If he is not an avid money-getter, as many are, he usually likes a comfortable income so that he can be free of worry to work and bring up a family. He may well have supralegalistic standards in some social matters. He may even split his life altogether and find great stability in the orthodoxy and ritual of an established church or synagogue. Many, like Einstein, find order in music or painting. And many researchers, far from living in an ivory tower, dedicate themselves to society through teaching and working against social injustice, invasions of private liberty, or racial discrimination in a way to show that what I have discussed as the religion of society inspires their full devotion.

All this, in one way or another, can be part of the religion of the new age. We partake of the modern age, however, insofar as we are seeking rather than affirming. I have used the word "agnosticism," but not in the negative sense that usually makes it a sneer in the nostrils of traditionalists. To accept the agnostic position does not mean that one must defend all agnostics, any more than to accept Catholicism one must defend the personal characters of popes Sixtus IV and Alexander VI. We all enjoy characterizing positions that we do not like in terms of their disreputable exponents. Agnosticism as a final dogma may well invite sneers. It is only a stimulus to search, which accepting any dogma as final is not. The true agnostic is not interested in whether man can "ever" know the truth as a whole. He sees little prospect of such an end, but is agnostic on that also. What he wants is to find out a little more than he knows now, and this the man who really thinks that he has the final answers cannot understand. Far from being a negative position, it is the greatest positive stimulus man has.

Wishful patterns can appear on the curtains of the scientists themselves. Their occupational disease is a tendency to paint their techniques and criteria, not as working hypotheses, but as final truth, deviation from which is almost a religious heresy. The idea that science exists only in those investigations that can use measurement and mathematics, for example, and that other types of approach are essentially "meaningless" is a dogma which bids fair to do great injury to the social sciences when used with uncritical devotion and harsh exclusion of other types of approach. Methods of history, psychoanalysis, cancer research, when taken as once for all established, can impede free investigation as sharply as any traditional theology. For example, the Hegelian dialectic and "economic interpretation," both brilliant new hypotheses in history and still of value, have become as destructive, as provocative of inquisitions, as any other dogmas. Even our methods must be working hypotheses.

Such a commitment to the quest for reality can never become "the religion of the future," since it can never be a popular one. Most people must have certainty in their creeds and ritualistic acts that promise to accomplish things. They will have their religion in the forms described in the previous chapter, so as to be snugly wrapped away from the chills of the tremendum. But increasingly the quest will become the way millions of trained minds continue in religion. The world has nothing to fear from it and much to hope.

Epilogue

As I close this little study, I hope that the reader has been impressed with the varieties of response man has made and can still make to the great Unknown of which he is a part. We could go on from this to all the fantastic diversities of the world's myths and rituals, but they would all fall, I believe, into the categories that we have been describing, as even the category of the agnostic search finally did. The divisions commonly suggested by those who discuss religion have, however, largely disappeared: that is, the absolute distinctions between God and man, the Infinite and the finite, the sacred and the profane, the eternal soul and the temporal body, and even right and wrong as distinctions we can finally know. Useful as they all can be on occasion and in some types of thinking, these distinctions are all creations of man with no identifiable objective reality.

I admire the tolerance of pagan antiquity, which recognized that people of one temperament or level of intelligence will find their security in religious experiences that have little meaning to others. Religious tolerance is of the greatest importance, since to attack other peoples' basic patterns, to destroy their curtains or rob them of the right to explore for themselves, so inundates them with the tremendum that they become utterly distraught or murderously vindictive. It is quite common that adolescents do this as they throw off the harness of childhood and come into the new world of experience and learning. Parents are usually disturbed enough about this. But we adults must not force our ideas on other mature people who by thought or thoughtlessness have accepted a pattern of life that we do not like ourselves. The ancients were tolerant enough until they believed that Anaxagoras and Socrates were attacking the gods painted on their curtains or until Judaism and, even more, Christianity faced them with militant intolerance. In the diversity of the modern world, however, especially of the One World, the anthropologist, psychologist, sociologist, diplomat, and pastor must each understand all the types here described and why they are important, to the point that he can enter into all these thought worlds with an appreciation of their several values and feel the impact even of what seem the most bizarre religious assertions.

We cannot avoid making value judgments about these patterns. It is not as though one pattern is as good as another. The god of the Aztecs, the religion of the Nazis, the petty particularism of fetishes, these seem to me to offer nothing but retardation for human development. If ethics is relative, we still cannot tolerate murder and rape. Marx has taught hundreds of millions that all the religious formulations of

men have been opiates, obstacles to human thought and social growth. His teaching itself quickly became one of the
world's most powerful opiates as it deadened his followers
to any real questioning. Is all religion, at least all blueprint
religion, an opiate? Religion can be more than that, but let
us be honest and admit that the paintings of any "truths" on
the curtains do lull us into a sense of security.

The "modern man" of whom I spoke in Chapter Five
may not want to be thus lulled, but he knows very well
that opiates have a tremendously important place in human
life. There is no reason in the world why we should endure
the physical agonies of surgery or death by cancer without
them. And we all must use spiritual opiates of religious illusion in one form or another. We need mythology, poetry,
music, philosophy, ethics, social loyalty, and security, and
one man cannot be creative in all. Here is true tolerance: not
that we shrug our shoulders and leave the deluded in their
delusions or forgive them their insuperable ignorance, but
that we by understanding can and do share in their points of
view. That way, the full life.

Index

personality of, 169; purpose of,
164–165; relation to, 108; and Sermon on the Mount, 107–108; special favors from, 18; Stoic idea
of, 38; as supreme law, 47; as
symbol, 180; will of, 134
Goethe, Johann Wolfgang von, 161
good, in Aristotle, 36; virtue and,
43
grace, 150
Greeks, aestheticism of, 135; knowledge as virtue among, 178; legalism of, 91; nakedness among,
80; religion of, 20–21; supralegalism of, 112–113
Greek tragedy, 89
guilt, 24–25, 69–70, 73; of Abraham,
82; conversion and, 149; God
and, 133; and Oedipus complex,
77–78; Paul's idea of, 60; salvation
and, 83; sex and, 71–72; wickedness and, 150

harmony, proportion and, 45–46
hate, 26
healthy-mindedness, 78, 102
Hegel, Georg Wilhelm Friedrich,
127
hell, guilt and, 70
Heraclitus, 51, 157, 162
heresy, 120, 123–124
Herman, Nicolas, 156 n.
Hesiod, 5, 112
Hindemith, Paul, 136
Hinduism, 8–9, 86, 148, 157
historical event, definition of, 169
Hitler, Adolf, 20, 23, 49, 117, 124,
173
Homer, 15
homosexuality, 78
hope, Christianity and, 84
human race, origin of, 166–167
Hume, David, 121
humility, security of, 4
Huxley, Julian, 76

id, 8, 66, 70, 73, 85, 117
idealism, 127, 134
identity, loss of, 157

Ignatius of Loyola, 150
ignorance, 6–7, 24, 28
illusion, need for, 177
immortality, 167
incest taboo, 71
individuality, 8
Infinite, the, 34
insanity, 15–16
instinct, reason and, 44
intelligence, 45, 115
Isaac, 80–81
Isis, 51
Islam, 2, 120, 148, 170

James, William, 2, 74–75, 78, 102,
160
Jehovah's Witnesses, 120
Jesus, 4, 10, 51, 60–62, 69, 74, 102–
103, 105, 126; death and resurrection of, 59; as Great Mother, 154–
156; as ideal, 149; as incarnate
Logos, 169; mysticism and, 152–
155; Paul's concept of, 59; prayer
and, 11; and sacraments, 143; salvation through, 82–84; as son of
God, 170; teachings of, 105–111
Jews, 95, 97–98, 111–113, 118, 128;
see also Judaism
John, 79, 83
John Chrysostom, 61
John of the Cross, 153
Judaism, 2, 22, 82, 90, 95, 128, 153,
185; Hellenistic, 31, 41; mystical,
81; supraorthodoxy and, 126–127;
Torah and, 93
Jung, Carl Gustav, 37, 65, 117
justice, integration and, 33

Khrushchev, Nikita S., 21
Kierkegaard, Sören, 131–135
killing, law against, 106
kindness, 111, 114
king, as sovereign, 47, 49, 92
Kipling, Rudyard, 98
knowledge, versus Darkness, 158;
and modern man, 161; in Stoic
philosophy, 39–40; tree of, 79;
virtue as, 39, 43, 178
kosher laws, 92